Parking Requirements
for Shopping Centers

Summary Recommendations
and Research Study Report

Second Edition

A Survey Study Conducted by Walker Parking Consultants
under the Direction of ULI–the Urban Land Institute and
the International Council of Shopping Centers

Urban Land Institute

International Council
of Shopping Centers

About ULI–the Urban Land Institute

ULI–the Urban Land Institute is a nonprofit education and research institute that is supported and directed by its members. Its mission is to provide responsible leadership in the use of land in order to enhance the total environment.

ULI sponsors education programs and forums to encourage an open international exchange of ideas and sharing of experiences; initiates re-search that anticipates emerging land use trends and issues and proposes creative solutions based on that research; provides advisory services; and publishes a wide variety of materials to disseminate information on land use and development. Established in 1936, the Institute today has more than 15,000 members and associates from more than 50 countries representing the entire spectrum of the land use and development disciplines.

Richard M. Rosan
President

About the International Council of Shopping Centers

Founded in 1957, the International Council of Shopping Centers (ICSC) is the global trade association of the shopping center industry. Its 38,000 members in the United States, Canada, and more than 70 other countries include shopping center owners, developers, managers, marketing specialists, investors, lenders, retailers, and other professionals as well as academics and public officials. As the global industry trade association, ICSC links with more than 20 national and regional shopping center councils throughout the world.

John T. Riordan
President

Project Staff

Rachelle L. Levitt
*Senior Vice President, Policy and Practice
Publisher*

Gayle Berens
*Vice President, Real Estate Development
Practice*

Robert T. Dunphy
*Senior Resident Fellow, Transportation
Project Director*

Nancy H. Stewart
*Director, Book Program
Managing Editor*

Barbara de Boinville
Copy Editor

Betsy VanBuskirk
Art Director

Meg Batdorff
Graphic Artist

Jeanne Berger Design
Design/Layout

Diann Stanley-Austin
*Associate Director of Publishing
Operations*

Recommended bibliographic listing:
ULI–the Urban Land Institute and The International Council of Shopping Centers. *Parking Requirements for Shopping Centers,* Second Edition. Washington, D.C.: ULI–the Urban Land Institute, 1999.

ULI Catalog Number: P92
International Standard Book Number: 0-87420-828-9
Library of Congress Catalog Card Number: 99-66868

Copyright 1999 by ULI–the Urban Land Institute
1025 Thomas Jefferson Street, N.W.
Suite 500 West
Washington, D.C. 20007-5201

Second Printing, 2000

Acknowledgments

This publication represents a major cooperative venture between ULI and the International Council of Shopping Centers. I had the pleasure of working with an outstanding advisory committee drawn from both organizations, whose advice at every stage of the work has been invaluable. Special thanks are due to Michael Baker, assistant research director of ICSC, whose counsel and humor helped spread the burden of managing this undertaking. Such a significant undertaking required the active involvement of the top management of each organization, and we appreciate the support of Dr. John Konarski III, senior vice president, ICSC, and Rachelle Levitt, senior vice president, policy and practice, ULI. The survey of parking characteristics, the most extensive ever conducted in the United States, would not have been possible without the voluntary participation of the shopping center managers, who collected the information, as well as those specifically identified in the case studies, who provided further information and graphics.

This study was conducted at the busiest time of the year for managers, and we acknowledge the extensive help of the committee chair, Kemper Freeman, who contacted executives of the management companies. The data were collected, interpreted, and reported by the study consultant, Walker Parking Consultants. Our primary contacts were John W. Dorsett, principal and director of study services, with cooperation from Pat Gibson at Kaku Associates, Inc. All members of the advisory committee reviewed the draft manuscript, and William Eager provided special technical assistance. In addition, we received comments from a major retail executive, Michael Lowenkron, vice president and director of real estate, JC Penney.

Finally, I would like to thank the ULI staff members instrumental in production, led by Nancy Stewart, Betsy Van-Buskirk, and Meg Batdorff, as well as Karrie Underwood, who incorporated all the changes in the manuscript.

Robert T. Dunphy

Advisory Committee for Parking Requirements for Shopping Centers

Contents

Contents (*cont.*)

Contents (*cont.*)

CHAPTER

1

Introduction

The Changing Face of Shopping Centers

The face of the regional shopping center in the United States has been changing. Retail shopping centers are getting larger. According to the International Council of Shopping Centers (ICSC) publication *Shopping Centers Today*, in 1965, only 73 shopping centers in the United States exceeded 800,000 square feet of gross leasable area (GLA), "the total floor area designed for the tenants' occupancy and exclusive use."[1] By 1974, that number had grown to 249. In 1998, more than 714 centers exceeded 800,000 square feet. In fact, 395 centers exceeded 1 million square feet—almost twice the size of shopping centers that were once considered large.

Not only is the size of centers changing. The mix of land uses within regional shopping centers also is different today. Retail entertainment centers are becoming more common. Retail centers of all sizes contain larger proportions of restaurant service, cinema, and entertainment venues. Moreover, relatively new types of shopping centers have evolved, such as power centers, theme centers, and fashion/specialty centers.

Nearly 20 years have passed since ICSC and the Urban Land Institute collected data for their 1980 study, also entitled

Parking Requirements for Shopping Centers. Since then, there have been a number of changes in shopper and industry characteristics that have affected parking needs. These include: increased labor force participation among women; higher levels of traffic congestion; growing specialization of the shopping center industry and the emergence of new retail formats; and the addition of entertainment to traditional centers. In light of these many changes, now is an appropriate time to update the study.

The primary goal of this current study is to recommend parking demand ratios for shopping centers in the United States, based upon observations of parking at existing centers. To achieve this objective, the study collected and evaluated data on a wide range of factors influencing travel behavior and parking demand at shopping centers. The findings were prepared in a format usable for all those interested in shopping center parking managers, owners, developers, designers, planners, and local officials.

This analysis updates two extensive studies on parking demand at shopping centers. The first study measured parking demand from 1973 to 1975 during the holiday peaks (the month of December). The results were reported

in the May 1977 issue of *Urban Land.* The second study analyzed data collected in 1980; it was sponsored by ICSC and published by ULI in 1982. Data from both of these studies will be compared with data collected during the holiday shopping season of 1998.

This Report

Data for this report were collected in two parts. First, an extensive questionnaire was distributed to shopping centers across the United States. Responses to the questionnaire were received from 490 centers. Second, responding centers were asked to participate in parking accumulation counts during the 1998 holiday season. Parking counts were conducted at 169 centers.

Every effort was made to obtain a reasonable sample size for each type and size of shopping center that was analyzed. Where data are limited, a word of caution is noted. For example, a very limited amount of data was collected for factory outlet centers, power centers, and fashion/specialty centers, so parking demand was not reported. Moreover, a limited amount of parking accumulation data was collected for neighborhood and community centers. Consequently, the recommendations contained in this report err on the conservative side for neighborhood and community centers.

This study features significantly more data for regional and super regional centers, for which parking is more of an issue. Survey data indicate that 18 percent of centers with less than 400,000 square feet reported that they experienced "ten or more" days annually in which parking occupancy exceeded 85 percent. In comparison, 45 per-cent of centers containing 600,000 to 1,499,999 square feet reported parking occupancies that exceeded 85 percent ten or more days of the year.

Chapters 3 and 4 of this report provide detail on the methodology used. Chapter 5 describes the general data collection results. In Chapters 6 and 7, the parking ratio recommendations are presented. The results of the General Questionnaire are provided in Chapters 8 and 9. Chapter 10 summarizes a series of case studies, and the appendices include all of the survey forms, in addition to the comprehensive matrix of recommended parking ratios.

Notes

[1]   ULI–the Urban Land Institute, *Shopping Center Development Handbook* (Washington D.C.: ULI–the Urban Land Institute, 1985).

2

Key Recommendations

This report presents a set of base recommendations for parking supply based on center size and makeup. An analysis of the survey data shows that these independent variables do not significantly affect the required parking supply:

- Geographic area
- Urban versus suburban setting
- Large city versus small city.

On the other hand, the amount of parking needed at a shopping center is affected by these variables:

- Proportion of restaurant, cinema, and entertainment land uses
- Percent of nonauto travel to the center
- Treatment of employee parking during shopping peaks
- Size of the center.

Adjustment factors for these variables will be discussed later in the report.

Parking Ratio Recommendations

Table 1 shows the recommended number of parking spaces per 1,000 square feet of gross leasable area (GLA).

The table located in Appendix A provides a comprehensive matrix of rec-

ommended ratios. This recommended provision of parking spaces will provide the typical shopping center with sufficient parking to serve the parking needs of customers and employees at the 20th busiest hour of the year. Moreover, these recommended ratios provide for a surplus of parking spaces during all but 19 hours of the more than 3,000 hours per year during which a shopping center is open. During 19 hours of each year, which are typically distributed over four peak shopping days, some patrons will not be able to find vacant spaces when they first enter the center. The recommended parking ratios are applicable for centers in which retail shops occupy at least 80 percent of the GLA.

The recommended parking ratios in Table 1 exclude centers in which 20 percent or more of occupied GLA is composed of restaurants, entertainment, and/or cinema space. The appropriate number of spaces for these centers should be determined using methodology such as that described in the Urban Land Institute's 1983 publication entitled *Shared Parking*. It defines shared parking as "parking spaces that can be used to serve two or more individual land uses without conflict or encroachment." Also, the data analyzed in this study suggest that for neighborhood and community centers, the recommended ratio may be as low as 3.7 spaces per 1,000 square feet of GLA provided

Table 1 Recommended Parking Ratios[a]			
	Percentage of GLA in Restaurant, Entertainment, and/or Cinema Space		
Center Size (GLA in Square Feet)	0–10%	11–20%[b]	>20%
Less than 400,000	4.0	4.0	Shared parking[d]
400,000–599,999	4.0–4.5 sliding scale[c]	4.0–4.5 sliding scale[c]	Shared parking[d]
600,000 and over	4.5	4.5	Shared parking[d]

a   Parked cars per 1,000 square feet of gross leasable area.

b   For each percent above 10 percent, a linear increase of 0.03 spaces per 1,000 square feet should be calculated.

c   Recommended parking ratio increases/decreases proportionally with center's square footage.

d   Shared parking is defined as parking spaces that can be used to serve two or more individual land uses without conflict or encroachment.

that additional spaces are available for restaurants, entertainment, and/or cinema use. However, because of limited parking data from these centers, the recommended parking ratio of 4.0 spaces per 1,000 square feet from the 1980 study should still be used.

As shown in Table 1, when restaurants, entertainment, and cinema space combine to equal 11 to 20 percent of the total GLA, a linear increase of 0.03 spaces per 1,000 square feet for each percent above 10 percent should be calculated. For instance, a 300,000-square-foot center in which restaurants, entertainment, and cinema space account for 14 percent of the total GLA would require 4.12 parking spaces per 1,000 square feet.

Base Level:	4.0 (Spaces)
+ 4% excess restaurant, entertainment, cinema x .03 =	.12
Estimated ratio:	4.12

For recommended ratios with a sliding scale, the parking ratio increases or decreases proportionally with the center's square footage. For example, a 500,000-square-foot center with restaurant, entertainment, and cinema space constituting 10 percent or less of the total GLA would require 4.25 spaces per 1,000 square feet (halfway between the 400,000- and 599,999-square-foot ratios).

Method of Travel
The method of travel influences parking demand at a center. Employees or customers who arrive by modes of transportation other than private automobile reduce the demand for parking.

The parking ratio recommendations contained in this report are for centers that are primarily auto dependent, with minimal walk-in or transit use.

Employee Parking Requirements
Parking demand for employees continues to account for approximately 20 percent of the total parking demand during the peak period. Thus, centers that require employees to park off site during the peak season could see up to a 20 percent reduction in the parking demand. However, this adjustment should be utilized with caution since centers with uncontrolled free parking often have difficulty completely enforcing employee parking.

Parking Supply Ratios
It is important in recommending parking ratios to determine the current parking supply. A series of parking supply ratios was calculated for centers with parking accumulation counts based on the number of parking spaces per 1,000 square feet. As seen in Table 2, the parking supply exceeded demand for the

survey period for all center sizes. Therefore, parking demand during the design hour was not constricted by the availability of parking.

Parking Space Design
In the 1970s and 1980s, there was a trend toward smaller vehicle sizes. As stated in the 1980 *Parking Requirements for Shopping Centers*, the expectation was "that by 1990, most automobiles (60 to 95 percent) in use nationwide would be compacts." However, according to the National Parking Association (NPA), vehicles became increasingly larger in the 1990s. This trend has accelerated with the increased sales of sport utility vehicles. The NPA's last report that detailed trends in car size was published in 1996. It stated that only 39 percent of vehicles on the road were considered compact. *Dimensions of Parking*, published by ULI, provides historical automobile sales data by size of vehicle.

Given the declining number of compact vehicles, a one-size-fits-all ("universal" stall) parking space design is recommended.

Table 2
Parking Supply and Demand Ratios for Centers with Car Counts

Center Size (GLA in Square Feet)	Number of Responses	Parking Ratio (Parking Spaces per 1,000 Square Feet of Occupied GLA)	
		Supply	Demand
Less than 400,000	49	5.8	3.7
400,000–599,999	15	5.6	4.0
600,000–1,499,999	96	5.8	4.5
1,500,000–2,500,000	9	4.7	3.8
Total	**169**		

A Comparison of 1980 and 1998 Studies

The recommended parking ratios for centers under 400,000 square feet are consistent in the 1980 and the 1998 studies. However, larger centers require lower parking ratios today than those recommended in 1980. This is particularly evident in centers with 600,000 square feet or more. Table 3 compares the findings of the 1980 and 1998 studies.

Table 3
Recommended Parking Ratios: 1980 and 1998 Studies

Center Size (GLA in Square Feet)	Parking Ratio (Parking Spaces per 1,000 Square Feet of Occupied GLA)	
	1980 Study	1998 Study
Less than 400,000	4.0	4.0
400,000–599,999	4.0	4.0–4.5 (sliding scale)
600,000 and over	4.0–5.0 (sliding scale)	4.5

Note: See Table 1 explanation of sliding scale.

CHAPTER 3

Study Methodology

Questionnaire

An extensive parking questionnaire was distributed to centers of varying types and sizes across the United States. The intent of the questionnaire was to determine the general parking characteristics of shopping centers, ascertain current industry parking practices, and solicit comments on the status of parking in the centers.

The General Questionnaire is presented in Appendix B and the responses in Appendix C. Nearly 500 centers responded to the questionnaire.

Parking Accumulation Counts

The questionnaire asked centers if they were willing to participate in the collection of parking accumulation data during the 1998 holiday peak. One hundred sixty-nine centers indicated a willingness to participate. A survey team was developed to conduct these accumulation counts for a specified time and date. For approximately 35 centers, these counts were obtained via aerial photographs. Detailed instructions were provided so that the data collection process would be consistent across the country. Chapter 4 explains how the time and dates for the collection of parking accumulation counts were chosen.

Of the 169 counts, 95 percent were conducted on December 12, 1998, between the hours of 1:00 p.m. and 3:00 p.m., while the remaining 5 percent were conducted on December 19 during the same hours.

Data Analysis

Responses to the questionnaires were analyzed by center size, location, and type. Cross tabulation of the responses was used to investigate the similarities and differences between the various sizes and types of centers.

In order to calculate a parking ratio, the parking count data were plotted on a graph showing center size and number of parked cars. Both linear and nonlinear regression analyses were performed on the data plots to determine the best fit of the data. A number of different groupings of the center sizes were analyzed to make sure that variation in the groupings did not change the recommended parking ratio.

The 1998 data were compared with the 1975 and 1980 survey results.

CHAPTER 4

Determining the 20th Highest Hour

Definition of Peak Hours

Previous studies have established the 20th highest hour of the year as the appropriate hour for determining parking requirements. *Parking Requirements for Shopping Centers,* published in 1980, gave this rationale:

This study has selected the 20th highest hour of the year as the demand hour upon which the design of shopping center parking facilities should be based. Use of this hour as the design period will result in adequate parking for all patrons and employees during the more than 3,000 hours per year a center is open. In fact, based on this design period, it is estimated that during 40 percent of the hours of the year, over half of the available spaces will be empty. However, during 19 hours of each year, distributed over ten days, some patrons will be unable to find parking spaces immediately upon entering a center.

Designing a shopping center parking facility to accommodate parking conditions during the average hour of demand would be unacceptable, since by definition, during half of the time parking would be inadequate. However, providing sufficient parking to meet conditions generated during a center's busiest hour of the year would result in substantial excess capacity during all but one hour of the year—an unrealistic design standard for the community, the consumer, and the shopping center developer/owner. This study again recommends the 20th highest hour of the year as the appropriate standard.

Selection of Survey Day and Time

Selection of the appropriate survey day and hour required evaluation of extensive data available from a limited number of centers, responses from the questionnaires, consistency with previous studies, and industry judgment. An array of electronic counting devices makes it possible to count pedestrians at entrances and exits, vehicle traffic on entry roads, and the number of

vehicles parking in paid facilities. Pedestrian or vehicle traffic data were available on a daily basis from 32 centers. Another 16 centers collected data on an hourly basis, offering around-the-clock tabulations of shopping center patrons throughout the year. An analysis of the detailed pedestrian and traffic data, shown in Appendix J, determined that the afternoon of December 12, 1998, between the hours of 1:00 p.m. and 3:00 p.m., had the best chance of approximating the 20th highest hour for the study's parking accumulation counts. This survey period also was the same as that used for the 1980 study. Although December 19th was used as a backup data collection day in the event of severely inclement weather or staff shortages, only 5 percent of the parked car data was collected on that day.

CHAPTER

5

Survey Results

The base data analyzed for this study were obtained from two surveys. The first—the General Questionnaire—contained questions regarding the profile and parking characteristics of each center. The second—the Parked Car Survey—studied parked vehicles on the survey date and time selected to approximate the 20th busiest hour. The General Questionnaire was distributed to a large number of centers; the Parked Car Survey focused on fewer centers.

General Questionnaire
Initial attempts were made to select centers randomly from a database of over 3,000 shopping centers. This database was believed to be representative of shopping centers within the United States. Once the sample was selected, the survey process began. This process produced far fewer completed surveys than anticipated. Therefore, a second approach was employed.

This second approach involved eliciting the support of top management of shopping center developers. Once this top management support was established, developers selected a representative sample of their centers for inclusion in the survey. Developers were asked for a specific number of centers —typically 10 to 20 percent of their portfolio. The purpose of this sampling

process was to select centers of various types located in different geographical areas. This approach produced nearly 500 completed questionnaire surveys.

Parked Car Survey
A one-time count of parked cars was conducted at 169 centers. The counts were acquired through a manual survey of the lots as well as aerial photographs taken of some centers. These counts were essential in developing parking ratios based on each center's square footage. (A parking ratio is defined as the number of parked cars per 1,000 square feet of occupied GLA.)

The Parked Car Survey had four components: the total number of on-site parking spaces; the number of vehicles that were illegally parked (including vehicles parked in areas without any striping, on grass, and in any other space outside of the marked parking spaces); the number of empty parking spaces; and the number of employee vehicles parked off site.

By adding the on-site parking capacity, the number of illegally parked cars, and the number of employees parking off site, and then subtracting the number of empty parking spaces, the total number of parked cars for each shopping center was calculated.

Definition of Center Types
The Urban Land Institute and the International Council of Shopping Centers define a shopping center as a group of retail and other commercial establishments that are planned, developed, and managed as a single property. Shopping centers are further classified for this survey into the following eight major categories:

Neighborhood center—The typical square footage for this type of center is about 30,000 to 100,000 or more. It usually includes a supermarket and/or drugstores.

Community center—Typically, this center type contains 100,000 to 350,000 square feet or more. Anchors usually consist of general merchandise stores, convenience stores, and occasionally large specialty/discount apparel stores.

Regional center—These centers have approximately 400,000 to 800,000 square feet. Department stores are the most common anchors. Regional centers customarily are enclosed.

Super regional center—Super regional centers are similar to regional centers. However, with over 800,000 square feet, they are larger than regional centers and usually have more department stores and a wider variety and assortment of stores than regional centers have.

Fashion/specialty center—At about 80,000 to 250,000 square feet or more, these centers tend to be high end and fashion oriented.

Power center—Power centers can have from 250,000 to 600,000 square feet. They usually include more category-dominant anchors, such as home improvement stores.

Theme/entertainment center—These centers, usually 80,000 to 250,000 square feet, are mainly leisure and tourist oriented.

Factory outlet center—Factory outlet centers can have anywhere from 50,000 to 400,000 square feet. Anchors at these centers typically are limited to manufacturers' outlet stores.

Response
Table 4 shows the 169 responses from the Parked Car Survey by size of center. From this data, ratios of parked cars per 1,000 occupied square feet (parking demand) were calculated.

Parking supply per 1,000 square feet of occupied GLA was also calculated.

Figures 1 and 2 show the distribution of parked car counts and questionnaire responses by center size.

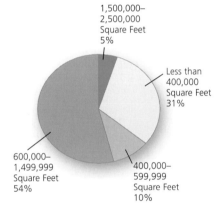

Figure 1
Parked Car Counts by Center Size

1,500,000–2,500,000 Square Feet 5%
Less than 400,000 Square Feet 31%
600,000–1,499,999 Square Feet 54%
400,000–599,999 Square Feet 10%

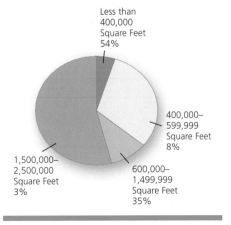

Figure 2
Questionnaire Responses by Center Size

Less than 400,000 Square Feet 54%
400,000–599,999 Square Feet 8%
600,000–1,499,999 Square Feet 35%
1,500,000–2,500,000 Square Feet 3%

As noted earlier, shopping centers are usually classified as specific center types based on total square footage, configuration, and store types. For this study, the respondents reported their center's square footage and type per a definition sheet included with the General Questionnaire. In most cases, the total square footage and tenant composition matched the appropriate definition. For example, most neighborhood centers had less than 100,000 square feet, with a supermarket or drugstore as the anchor tenant. Moreover, most centers classifying themselves as super regional contained more than 800,000 square feet and were anchored by department stores. However, there were a few exceptions, and in those cases the responses were edited by the consultant.

Geographic Coverage
The study is limited to shopping centers in the United States. Shopping centers from 46 states and the District of Columbia participated in the study by completing a General Questionnaire. (Alaska, Montana, North Dakota, and Wyoming had no centers that participated.) The hourly/daily counts were conducted at 32 centers in 21 states. A large number of car counts was obtained from centers in California and Texas, with 36 and 29 center surveys acquired, respectively. Arizona was represented with car counts at 11 centers, and the remaining states all had fewer than ten participants.

These responses reflect the underlying distribution of centers in those states. According to the National Research Bureau, California had 5,887 centers

Table 4 Centers by Size with Car Counts	
Center Size (GLA in Square Feet)	Number of Responses
Less than 250,000	38
250,000–399,999	14
400,000–599,999	17
600,000–799,999	30
800,000–1,199,999	48
1,200,000 and greater	22
Total	**169**

in 1998—nearly twice as many centers as in the next highest state, Florida, which had 3,278 centers. Texas ranked third with 2,976 centers. Table 5 shows the geographic distribution of centers participating in the study by state. A map showing the location of the participating centers is included in Appendix H.

Table 6 classifies each state and the District of Columbia into ten regions. The first column lists the number of centers from each region that completed a General Questionnaire. The next column shows each region's responses as a percentage of the total number of responses provided for all regions combined. The third column gives the actual number of existing shopping centers for each region. The final column gives each region's centers as a percentage of the total existing centers in the United States. This table shows that the geographic distribution of participating centers is virtually the same as the distribution of all centers nationwide.

Table 5
Centers Participating in General Questionnaire, Parking Accumulation Counts, and Parked Car Surveys, by State[a]

State	Participated in General Questionnaire	Completed Parking Accumulation Counts	Provided Daily Traffic Data
Alabama	13	0	0
Alaska	0	0	0
Arizona	16	11	2
Arkansas	2	1	0
California	61	37	3
Colorado	6	2	1
Connecticut	3	0	0
Delaware	1	0	0
District of Columbia	1	0	0
Florida	30	6	2
Georgia	24	5	2
Hawaii	5	0	0
Idaho	2	0	0
Illinois	18	8	0
Indiana	3	2	2
Iowa	2	0	0
Kansas	8	3	0
Kentucky	3	1	0
Louisiana	6	0	0
Maine	5	0	0
Maryland	9	4	0
Massachusetts	7	4	0
Michigan	8	3	3
Minnesota	6	4	1
Mississippi	6	0	0
Missouri	9	2	1
Montana	0	0	0
Nebraska	11	0	0
Nevada	5	4	0
New Hampshire	5	1	0
New Jersey	6	3	1
New Mexico	5	1	0
New York	20	8	1
North Carolina	18	3	1
North Dakota	0	0	0
Ohio	13	5	1
Oklahoma	5	3	1
Oregon	6	0	0
Pennsylvania	21	2	1
Rhode Island	1	0	0
South Carolina	12	1	1
South Dakota	1	0	0
Tennessee	16	5	0
Texas	58	29	3
Utah	2	1	1
Vermont	3	0	0
Virginia	12	6	2
Washington	11	2	1
West Virginia	3	1	0
Wisconsin	2	1	1
Wyoming	0	0	0
Total	**490**	**169**	**32**

a   Including District of Columbia.

Table 6
Regional Distribution of Participating Centers

Region	States	Number of Centers Completing General Questionnaire	Region's Responses as % of Total Responses	Actual Number of Centers in Each Region[a]	Region's Centers as % of Total Centers
1	Connecticut, Maine, Massachusetts, New Jersey, New Hampshire, Rhode Island Vermont	30	6%	3,729	9%
2	Delaware, New York, Pennsylvania	42	9%	3,509	8%
3	District of Columbia, Maryland, North Carolina, South Carolina, Virginia, West Virginia	55	11%	4,810	11%
4	Alabama, Florida, Georgia, Mississippi, Tennessee	89	18%	7,114	16%
5	Indiana, Kentucky, Michigan, Ohio	27	6%	4,243	10%
6	Iowa, Minnesota, Montana, North Dakota, South Dakota, Wisconsin	11	2%	1,643	4%
7	Illinois, Kansas, Missouri, Nebraska	46	9%	3,271	8%
8	Arkansas, Louisiana, Oklahoma, Texas	71	14%	4,614	11%
9	Arizona, Colorado, Idaho, Nevada, New Mexico, Utah, Wyoming	36	7%	2,866	7%
10	Alaska, California, Hawaii, Oregon, Washington	83	17%	7,402	17%
	Totals	**490**	**100%**	**43,201**	**100%**

a   Data for this column from ICSC, *Shopping Centers Today, 1998.*

6

Parking Demand

The completed parking counts collected by field survey and aerial photographs were linked to square footage data to develop parking ratios. These parking ratios are summarized for informational purposes for each of the major shopping center types represented. Statistical analysis was then performed to examine some of the key variables found to influence parking demand, as well as those found not to have an apparent impact.

Center Type

Average peak parking demands found in the 1998 survey are shown in Table 7,

along with the median (half have higher demand, half have lower demand), and the range observed for that type of center. The parking ratio was not calculated for categories with fewer than three samples, deemed an inadequate number.

The 1980 study was made up entirely of neighborhood, community, super regional, and regional centers. Since then, there has been an emergence of new center types; theme/entertainment, power, fashion/specialty, and factory outlet centers, which are all represented in the current survey. In 1980, neighborhood and community centers accounted

for 62 percent of the response distribution. In 1998, however, super regional and regional centers accounted for 64 percent of the response (Figure 3).

The four most common type of shopping centers were represented most frequently and are summarized in more detail. The data covers all centers, including those with significant proportions of restaurants, entertainment, and/or cinema space, for which adjustments are discussed below.

Twelve neighborhood centers completed surveys. The lowest peak parking

		Parking Ratio (Parked Cars per 1,000 Square Feet of Occupied GLA)				
Center Type	Number of Centers Responding	Low	Median	Average	High	Standard Deviation
Neighborhood[a]	12	2.3	3.0	3.3	4.5	0.7
Community[a]	19	1.3	4.0	3.7	6.3	1.3
Regional	38	2.4	4.5	4.5	6.4	1.2
Super Regional	69	3.1	4.8	4.7	5.9	0.6
Fashion/Specialty	3	–	–	–	–	–
Power[a]	12	1.9	3.0	3.2	5.6	1.2
Theme/Entertainment[a]	12	1.5	3.6	3.5	6.4	1.2
Factory Outlet	3	–	–	–	–	–
Other	1	–	–	–	–	–
Total	**169**					

Table 7
Parking Ratios by Center Type

a   Use data with caution, sample size was small.

Note: No data are shown where dashes appear, as sample size was too small.

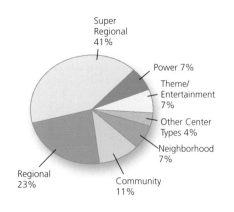

Figure 3
Distribution of Parked Car Counts by Center Type

Super Regional 41%
Power 7%
Theme/Entertainment 7%
Other Center Types 4%
Neighborhood 7%
Community 11%
Regional 23%

Note: The center types are defined in Chapter 5.

demand observed was 2.3 and the highest was 4.5. The average neighborhood center had 3.3 parked cars per 1,000 square feet of gross leasable area.

Figure 4 is a plot of each neighborhood center by occupied square feet of GLA (x-axis) and by the number of parked cars (y-axis).

Responses were received from 19 community centers. Peak parking demand ranged from 1.3 to 6.3 spaces per 1,000 square feet. The mean peak demand was 3.7 spaces, slightly higher than for neighborhood centers. Figure 5 is a plot of each community center by square feet of occupied GLA (x-axis) and by the number of parked cars (y-axis).

Regional centers, with 38 total responses, had a low and high parking ratio of 2.4 and 6.4, respectively, and an average of 4.5 parked cars per 1,000 square feet, significantly higher than for community centers. Figure 6 is a plot of each regional center by square feet of occupied GLA (x-axis) and by the number of parked cars (y-axis).

Super regional centers produced 69 responses. Their lowest parking ratio was 3.1, the highest was 5.9, and they had the overall highest average peak demand of all center types at 4.7 parked cars per 1,000 square feet. Figure 7 is a plot of each super regional center.

Power centers were represented with 12 completed surveys. The lowest ratio within this center type was 1.9, and the highest was 5.6. Power centers had the lowest observed peak parking demand at 3.2 parked cars per 1,000 square feet.

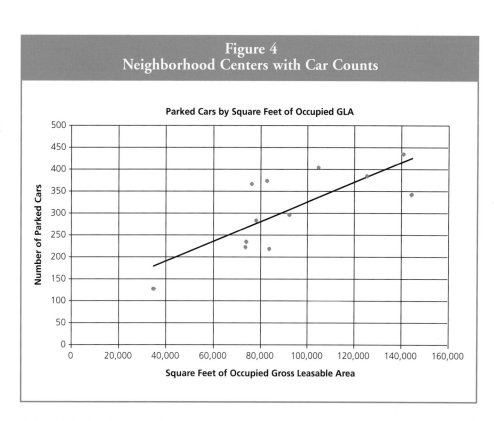

Figure 4
Neighborhood Centers with Car Counts

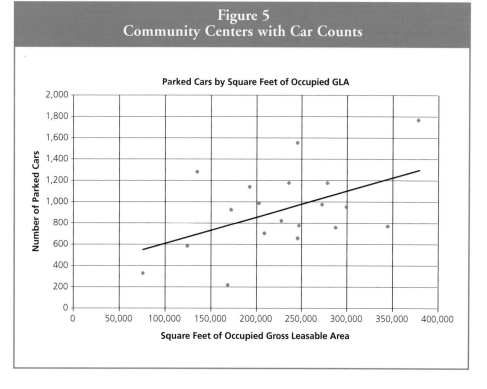

Figure 5
Community Centers with Car Counts

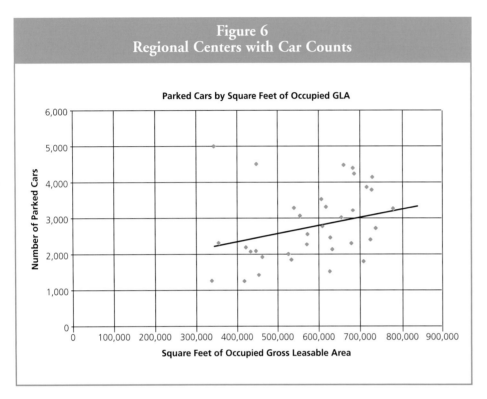

Figure 6
Regional Centers with Car Counts

Parked Cars by Square Feet of Occupied GLA

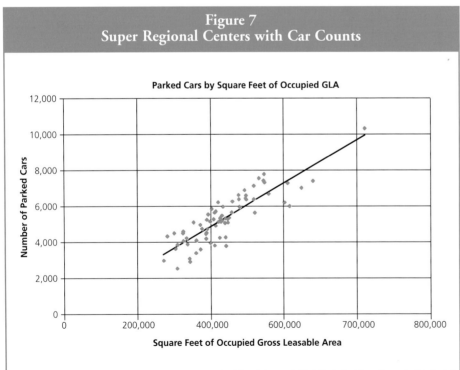

Figure 7
Super Regional Centers with Car Counts

Parked Cars by Square Feet of Occupied GLA

Theme/entertainment centers were also represented with 12 surveys. Parking ratios ranged from 1.5 to 6.4 parked cars per 1,000 square feet, with an average of 3.5 parked cars per 1,000 square feet. These parking demands are lower than those of community centers, which are probably the most comparable centers in terms of size. However, because of the small sample size, it is difficult to place too much confidence in these estimates of parking demand. Moreover, as indicated below, peak parking demands for theme/entertainment centers may occur outside the traditional peak season for retailing.

Only three fashion/specialty centers completed surveys, and only three responses were obtained from factory outlet centers. Because of the small sample size, no parking ratios were calculated for these two center types.

The next section of this report stratifies the parking accumulation data by center size, which is the basis of the key recommendations in this report.

Center Size
Table 8 provides a breakdown of the number of peak hour parked cars per 1,000 square feet by size of center. Mean parking ratios are provided as well as the observed ranges in demand. The ranges represent the lowest and highest parking ratios supplied by all of the centers. The mean ratio for a center size is the average size of all centers for a category of center size.

The usable responses from 169 centers included each center's total square

Table 8
Parking Ratios by Center Size: Centers with Cinema/Restaurant/Entertainment Space Less Than 21 Percent of GLA

Center Size (GLA in Square Feet)	Number of Responses	Parking Ratio (Parked Cars per 1,000 Square Feet of Occupied GLA)			
		Low	Average	High	Standard Deviation
Less than 400,000	41	1.3	3.7	6.4	1.1
400,000–599,999	14	2.4	4.1	5.6	0.9
600,000–1,499,999	95	2.1	4.6	6.4	0.9
1,500,000–2,500,000	8	3.2	4.0	4.7	0.5
	158				

footage. The lowest parking ratio for any responding center—1.3—occurred within the smallest center size range (under 400,000 square feet). Parking ratios above 6.0 were observed for each range of center size except for centers between 1,500,000 and 2,500,000 square feet.

Parking Requirements for Centers with Minimal Restaurant, Entertainment, and Cinema Space

Peak parking demand to accommodate the survey date selected, the second Saturday before Christmas, was found to vary with the size of the center and the amount of floor space devoted to restaurant, entertainment, and/or cinema space. For those with less than 11 percent of GLA used for those purposes, the following rates apply:

The recommended parking ratio for centers with less than 400,000 square feet is 4.0 spaces per 1,000 square feet as described in Table 1. The actual parking occupancy surveys conducted as part of this analysis found a slightly

lower parking ratio. However, it was decided not to use the lower ratio because of the relatively small sample size, the variety of different types of centers represented in this category, and the possibility that the centers experience parking peaks during other seasons. Only 41 retail centers meeting the criterion of containing at least 80 percent retail space were sampled, and the consensus was that this was not a large enough sample to adequately represent both the large number of centers and the wide diversity found in retail centers under 400,000 square feet.

These smaller centers could more easily contain a larger proportion of supermarkets, restaurants, cinemas, and nondepartment store type retail land uses than could larger centers. Thus they may experience their 20th highest design hour at a time other than the midday hours of one of the Saturdays before Christmas.

Because of the small sample size and the uncertainty over the actual identification of the design hour, the data did not present enough justification to modify the

4.0 spaces per 1,000 square feet ratio recommended in the 1980 study.

At centers with 400,000 to 599,000 square feet of GLA, the parking demand index increases from 4.0 to 4.5 in a linear progression as size increases. For example, a 500,000-square-foot center with restaurant, entertainment, and cinema space constituting 10 percent or less of the total GLA requires 4.25 spaces per 1,000 square feet (halfway between the 400,000- and 599,999-square-foot ratios).

Centers larger than 600,000 square feet, up to about 1.5 million square feet of GLA, require an average of 4.6 spaces per 1,000 square feet of GLA. The parking occupancy counts included eight centers in excess of 1.5 million square feet. The parking counts at these centers suggest that the parking ratio may decrease as centers exceed this threshold. Because of the small sample size, centers in excess of 1.5 million square feet were not placed in a separate category, but the ratio reduction is worth noting.

Adjustments for centers with a greater amount of space in restaurants, entertainment, and/or cinemas will be addressed in the next section.

Comparison of 1975, 1980, and 1998 Studies

The parking ratios have undergone a significant shift since the shopping center parking study published in the May 1977 issue of *Urban Land*. The ratios determined in that 1975 study resemble the ratios from the 1998 study quite

Figure 8
Retail Center Distribution: 1975

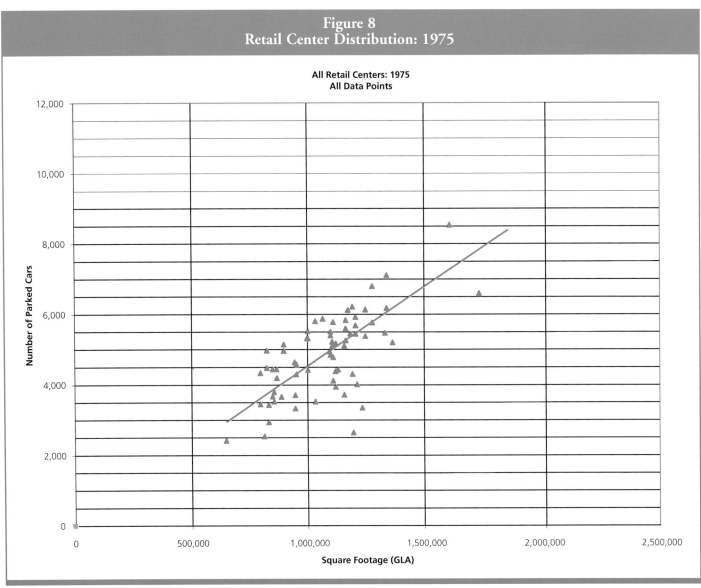

All Retail Centers: 1975
All Data Points

Source: *Urban Land* magazine, May 1977.

closely. However, the 1980 study determined higher parking ratios than did either this study or the 1975 study.

Figures 8, 9, and 10 present plots of each center that provided car counts for the 1975, 1980, and 1998 studies, respectively. Centers are classified and plotted by square footage (x-axis) and the number of parked vehicles (y-axis).

The 1975 study included only centers of 600,000 or more square feet. The linear regression for centers of this size was almost identical to the 1998 study.

However, the 1980 study displayed significantly higher parking ratios for larger shopping centers. A comparison of the current study's results with those of the 1980 study indicates a trend of proportionately decreasing parking ratios as centers larger than 600,000 square feet increase in size.

Figure 9
Retail Center Distribution: 1980

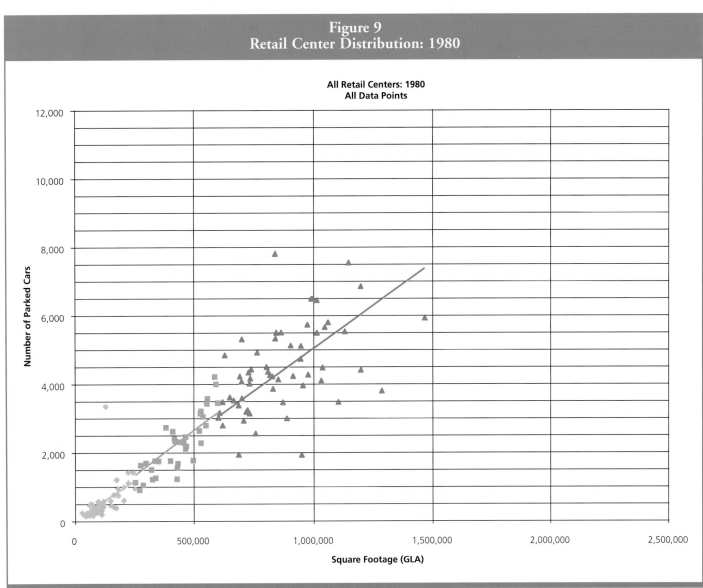

All Retail Centers: 1980
All Data Points

Source: Urban Land Institute, *Parking Requirements for Shopping Centers,* 1982.

Figure 10
All Retail Centers: 1998 Data Points

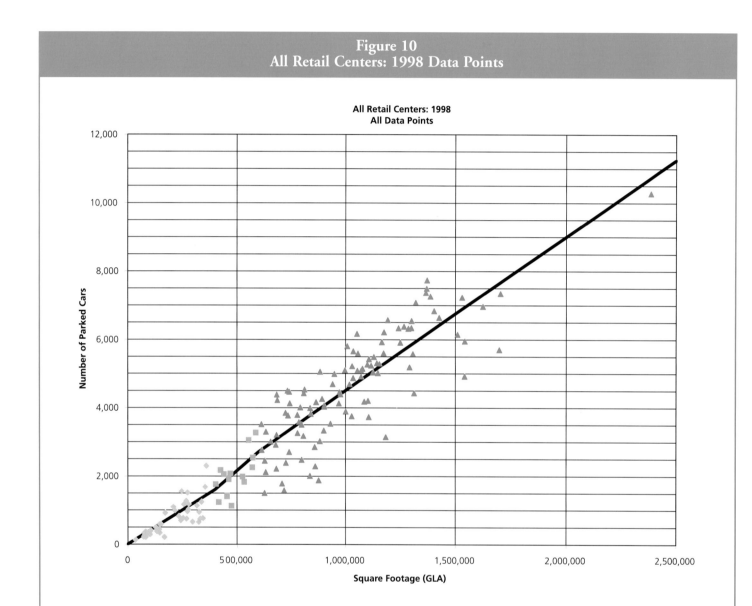

All Retail Centers: 1998
All Data Points

Source: ULI/ICSC Survey, 1998.

Special Considerations and Adjustments

Nonretail Uses

Nonretail land uses influence the over-all parking needs of a shopping center. The parking ratios recommended in the previous section are valid for centers where cinema, restaurant, and entertainment land uses are less than 11 percent of the total GLA.

For centers with combinations of restaurant plus entertainment plus cinema that constitute 11 to 20 percent of the center's GLA, a simple adjustment to the base ratio must be made (Table 9). A linear incremental increase of 0.03 spaces per 1,000 square feet for each percent above 10 percent will produce a parking supply adequate to handle this combination of land uses.

When the nonretail land uses exceed 20 percent of the center's GLA, the parking ratios recommended in Table 9 are no longer applicable. With these combinations of land uses, a special methodology is required, such as that found in the Urban Land Institute's *Shared Parking*. The *Shared Parking* methodology allows for an identification of the peak parking demand for different combinations of land uses.

For centers with large (20 percent or more of GLA) restaurant, entertainment, and cinema components, the peak parking demand may not occur

Center Size (GLA in Square Feet)	Parking Ratio (Parked Cars per 1,000 Square Feet of Occupied GLA)	
	Percentage of GLA in Restaurant, Entertainment, and/or Cinema Space	
	11–20%	>20%
Less than 400,000	4.0[a]	Shared parking
400,000–599,999	4.0–4.5 sliding scale[a]	Shared parking
600,000 and over	4.5[a]	Shared parking

**Table 9
Parking Ratio Adjustments**

a   For each percent above 10 percent, a linear increase of 0.03 spaces per 1,000 square feet should be calculated.
Note: Sliding scale and shared parking are defined in Table 1.

at the same time on Saturday as it does for more conventional retail-based regional shopping centers. Moreover, the peak parking demand at these types of centers may not even occur during the December holiday shopping period, but rather during weekends when the cinema activity is at its highest.

Table 10 shows parking demand at four centers on two Saturdays: one in December and the other in March. A majority of the floor area for two of these centers consisted of restaurant, entertainment, and/or cinema tenants. By comparison, less than 20 percent of the floor area in the other two centers was comprised of these tenants. At 8:00 p.m. on Saturday, March 27, 1998, the centers heavily occupied by the restaurant, entertain-

ment, and cinema tenants experienced significantly higher parking occupancy levels than did these same centers on Saturday, December 12, 1998. The two centers leasing less than 20 percent of their space to restaurant, entertainment, and cinema uses had higher parking occupancies on Saturday, December 12, 1998, than on March 27, 1998.

For example, at the 400,000-square-foot shopping center where 72 percent of the total GLA was occupied by restaurant, entertainment, and/or cinema uses, the parking occupancy counts differed markedly by season. The center was more than two-and-a-half times busier during a Saturday evening in March than during the afternoon of Saturday, December 12, 1998.

Cinemas with 12 to 30 screens were extremely rare in the mid-1980s when ULI's shared parking research was first conducted. The development pattern of cinemas has changed dramatically since then. The appendices of this report contain more updated data on the weekday/weekend peak demand, hourly and seasonal variation in cinema parking usage.

Table 10
Weekend Parking Demand for Four Centers, December and March 1998

Center Size (GLA in Square Feet)	Percentage of GLA Occupied by Restaurant, Entertainment, and Cinema Space	Percentage of 12/12/98 Demand		
		Sat. 12/12/98 1:00 p.m.	Sat. 3/27/1998 1:00 p.m.	8:00 p.m.
1,840,000	6%	100%	66%	19%
568,500	18%	100%	66%	85%
873,750	55%	100%	127%	143%
400,000	72%	100%	98%	253%

Nonautomobile Travel

The parking studies conducted in 1998 included counts at centers that were served primarily by automobile. In the vast majority of centers, 90 to 95 percent of shoppers arrived by automobile. Shopping centers with significant amounts of walk-in trade from nearby businesses or neighborhoods may require less parking, and these ratios can be adjusted proportionally. However, centers with 90 percent or more of their employees and patrons arriving by private vehicles require no adjustments to the peak demands reported here.

Employee Parking

Based on the data that centers provided for this study, parking demand by employees continues to make up approximately 20 percent of all parking demand during the peak period. At centers where employee parking is located off site during the peak season, parking demand could be 20 percent lower, thus helping to accommodate peak-period parking for customers.

Centers that have the ability to prohibit employee parking on site may be able to reduce the 20 percent employee parking considerably. For example, shopping centers that charge for parking and issue their employees key cards or passes allowing them entry to the parking facility could, with modern equipment, void the passes during the peak shopping season. Under this scenario, employees could be "forced" to park in the designated areas off site.

Centers that have uncontrolled, free parking may not be as successful at keeping employees parked off site. They can only encourage their employees to do so. The parking ratio reduction for those centers would be proportionally less.

Parking Lot Design

The trend in today's parking design is away from a mix of compact and full-size parking spaces and toward a universal, "one-size fits all" parking space dimension. This universal space has been shown to be an effective parking design technique. Not only are today's large cars smaller than those of the past, but the current mix of vehicles means it is likely that a large car will be parked next to a small car, providing an additional comfort margin. Shopping center parking design should take advantage of the universal space. The resulting parking lot would be more convenient for customers because no compact spaces would be abused or left vacant. Consequently, it would be a more efficient parking design (offering a higher number of effective parking spaces). *Dimensions of Parking* (published by ULI) more fully explores this trend.

Short-term parking facilities require a greater level of parking ease and convenience because the patron is making only a brief stop and is probably unfamiliar with the parking facility. Short-term parking locations usually require a greater parking angle and wider parking stalls and drive aisles. Such would be the case for shoppers at neighborhood convenience centers, for example. For longer-term parking, such as that needed for employees, the user generally is familiar with the facility and able to negotiate a tighter configuration.

8

Profile of Participating Centers

The General Questionnaire included four core components: "Information for This Center," "Parking at This Center," "Transit at This Center," and "Additional Data on This Center." A total of 490 questionnaires were acquired from center managers across the United States. The responses are summarized below. A complete presentation of the responses is included in Appendix C, General Questionnaire Results.

Shopping Center Location

The first question dealt with shopping center location; 483 participants responded to this question and seven left it unanswered. According to the responses, 39 percent of the centers were located in a suburban setting;

30 percent in an urban setting; and 23 percent, in a large urban area (population greater than 250,000). Only 6 percent classified their center as being in a rural/highway nonurban area, and an additional 2 percent were classified as "other."

Shopping Center Type

Shopping center types are defined in terms of square footage and anchor tenants (see Chapter 5). Of the 490 General Questionnaires received, 489 centers categorized their center type, and one center did not answer the question. Of the total responses, 28 percent were from neighborhood centers, 23 percent were from community centers, 21 percent were from super regional centers, and 15 percent were

from regional centers. These four center types represented an overwhelming majority of the participants.

The remaining five center types were found in a combined total of 12 percent of all respondents. Six percent of the questionnaires were returned from power centers, and fashion/specialty centers represented 2 percent of the total completed questionnaires. Respondents from an additional 2 percent of the centers stated they were factory outlet centers, and 1 percent believed that they fell into the "other" category. The smallest number of responses came from theme/entertainment centers, which constituted only 1 percent of all respondents.

9

Parking Characteristics of Participating Centers

The following section addresses parking operations and patterns for each of the shopping centers.

General Parking Characteristics

Overall, few shopping centers accommodated patrons with spaces in a parking garage or parking structure. In fact, 85 percent of the 490 centers did not have either of these parking configurations. Thirteen percent of the centers said they did have one of these types of parking facilities, and 2 percent did not answer the question.

Parking Fees and Validation

Patrons were rarely charged for parking. In 94 percent of the returned questionnaires, respondents indicated there was no parking charge to the customer. Only 2 percent of the centers verified a parking charge, while the remaining 4 percent left the question unanswered. All centers that did charge for parking were located in large urban areas.

Moreover, 86 percent of the centers did not have a parking validation program. Two percent did. This is logical since few centers charged for parking at all. The question was left unanswered by 12 percent of the respondents, presumably because they had no parking charge and thus felt the question was not applicable.

Valet parking was another rarity. Eighty-three percent of the shopping centers surveyed did not offer any type of valet parking program, whereas 4 percent did. The question was not answered by 13 percent of the respondents.

Managers' Views of Parking

Center managers were asked to record the number of days per year that on-site parking was fully occupied. Seventy-seven percent of all the responding centers based their response on general observation, while 12 percent based it on previous occupancy counts. Eleven percent of all centers did not clarify their basis for response. The most common response, from 43 percent of the centers, was that on-site parking was never fully occupied. However, 26 percent of the centers said that the parking lots were fully occupied at least ten or more days of the year, indicating a wide variance among the participating centers. About 18 percent of the centers believed parking was at capacity from four to nine days of the year, while the remaining centers (10 percent) had fully occupied parking from one to three days. Three percent did not answer the question. Table 11 provides a breakdown of the number of days that parking was fully occupied for each center size range.

Table 11 provides evidence that suggests that larger centers tend to have more problems with inadequate parking compared with smaller centers. For example, 58 percent of the centers with less than 400,000 square feet reported "never" experiencing a day when parking exceeded 85 percent occupancy. By comparison, only 14 percent of centers with 600,000 to 1,499,999 square feet reported "never" experiencing a day with capacity parking (above 85 percent occupancy). Moreover, 18 percent of centers with less than 400,000 square feet reported that they experienced "ten or more" days annually where parking occupancy exceeded 85 percent. Comparatively, 45 percent of centers with 600,000 to 1,499,999 square feet reported parking occupancies exceeding 85 percent ten or more days of the year.

Peak Demand

Following the question concerning the number of days during which on-site parking was fully occupied, center managers were asked if this peak parking demand was associated with a special event, seasonal/holiday activity, or a combination of both. Sixty-three percent responded that seasonal/holiday activity was the main reason for peak demand, whereas only 3 percent responded that special events created heavy demand. Twenty-two percent

Table 11
Annual Number of Days with Capacity Parking (Above 85 percent)

Center Size (GLA in Square Feet)	Number of Responses							
	Never	One	Two	Three	Four to Six	Seven to Nine	Ten or More	Total
Less than 400,000	170	9	7	16	26	14	53	**295**
400,000–599,999	15	0	3	3	5	1	10	**37**
600,000–1,499,999	18	1	9	8	26	9	58	**129**
1,500,000–2,500,000	0	0	1	2	1	1	3	**8**
Total	203	10	20	29	58	25	124	**469**

of the centers replied that it was a combination of both that spurred the fully occupied parking lots.

Center managers were asked to describe specific dates and/or circumstances in which peak demand occurred. Although many of these dates and circumstances varied, some of the more common responses were the following: weekends; holidays; day after Thanksgiving; weekends in December; days before forecasted snow; and back-to-school sales.

Transportation Management Associations

A transportation management association is an establishment that helps employers reduce traffic concentration and travel demand. Associations are usually formed in densely developed business districts with worsening roadway congestion. Few shopping centers that participated in the study took part in a local or regional transportation management association (only 11 percent), while 85 percent did not. Four percent of the centers did not answer the question.

Employee Parking

Eighty-seven percent of the centers surveyed allowed employees to park on site during off-peak seasons. Moreover, 66 percent indicated that there were no specific reserved spaces for employees. For the 34 percent that did offer reserved spaces, both the number and location of the spaces varied. Typically, however, the reserved spaces were located in remote lots and around the outer periphery of the property, allowing customers to have prime parking access to department stores and main entrances. Employees were charged for parking in only seven of the centers surveyed (1 percent). All seven centers also charged patrons to park, and each center was equipped with a parking structure. Six of the seven centers were located in a large urban setting, and the remaining center was situated in an urban setting. During peak shopping times, employees were asked to park in a different location, according to 36 percent of the returned questionnaires.

Handicapped Parking

Seventy-seven percent of the respondents had few problems with violation of handicapped parking; 17 percent felt that violations occurred with regularity. The question was not answered by 6 percent of the participants. Also, 77 percent of the respondents stated that there were no designated spaces for compact cars. (See Chapter 1 on parking implications of the compact car.)

Adjacent Land Use

Adjacent property and land use can have a significant impact on the parking needs of shopping centers. For example, heavy demand for parking on an adjacent property can produce overflow into a shopping center's parking lots, thus depleting the parking supply. Conversely, some shopping centers have been able to benefit from adjacent properties with a parking surplus during times of peak shopping. For one particular center, an adjacent office superstore had enough parking surplus to accommodate the shopping center's patrons during times of inadequate parking.

Parking Problems

Most shopping centers (73 percent) indicated that parkers from adjacent properties or land uses did not park frequently on their property. Six percent of the centers agreed that when this does happen, it significantly lessens parking availability for their shoppers. However, 75 percent of the centers left this second question unanswered.

Only 28 percent of all returned questionnaires answered whether or not any action had been taken to curb unauthorized parking. Eighteen percent agreed that some sort of action had been taken, whereas 10 percent said there had been no action taken. Those that had made an attempt to curb unauthorized parking had done so by means of:

- Ticketing
- Towing
- Written warnings
- Booting
- Signage.

In addition to parking problems caused by adjacent properties or land uses, centers reported the following parking problems:

- Poor lighting in lots
- Vehicles speeding through lots
- Difficulty educating customers that parking is available in other lots
- Fire lane violations
- Enforcing employee parking regulations
- Vehicles occupying more than one parking space
- Abandoned cars
- Snow removal
- Cleanliness
- Vandalism
- Traffic accidents.

Only 10 percent of all centers that returned the questionnaire had seen the need to increase their parking for reasons other than expansion of tenant floor size. Seventy-four percent said that an increase was not necessary, and 16 percent provided no answer.

Transit Service
Thirty-six percent of the responding centers had scheduled bus service to the shopping center area, a surprisingly high rate of transit access in light of the relatively negligible use of transit to most shopping centers. Five percent had scheduled train service. For all of the centers with scheduled bus service to the center property, the following amenities were provided for transit patrons:

- 75 percent provided a shelter or canopy
- 82 percent were equipped with seating
- 72 percent provided signage for bus schedules and routes
- 20 percent had an interior waiting area
- 31 percent had plantings
- 13 percent provided park-and-ride or commuter parking
- 1 percent arranged for connection to the transit system
- 9 percent indicated an amenity not included on the questionnaire.

Completed Questionnaires by Center Size
Overall, centers from each size range participated by completing a General Ques-

tionnaire. By far, centers under 400,000 square feet returned the greatest number of questionnaires. In fact, this size range constituted 44 percent of the total respondents for the study. Centers with 600,000 to 1,499,999 square feet were next with 29 percent of the total respondents. Seven percent of the respondents listed their center size between 400,000 and 599,999 square feet. Lastly, centers with 1,500,000 to 2,500,000 square feet constituted 2 percent of all the participating shopping centers.

Seventeen percent of the respondents did not report their total square footage. These figures are shown in Table 12.

Parking Supply
To determine whether parking demand during the design hour was constricted by the availability of parking, the number of parking spaces provided per 1,000 square feet—the parking supply —was evaluated.

The following parking supply ratios are figured for centers based on setting and

Table 12 Questionnaire Responses by Center Size		
Center Size (GLA in Square Feet)	Number of Centers Responding	Proportion of Respondents
Less than 400,000	218	44%
400,000–599,999	33	7%
600,000–1,499,999	142	29%
1,500,000–2,500,000	12	2%
Subtotal	405	83%
Not answered	85	17%
Total	**490**	**100%**

24

type; they include the extreme low and high, as well as the average, for each center type.

The parking supply ratios were first examined in terms of center type. Community centers provided the lowest number of parking spaces per 1,000 square feet (4.7); theme/entertainment and factory outlet centers provided the highest number of spaces (5.4 each). The sample size for the theme/entertainment and factory outlet centers was small so the findings should be viewed with caution. Parking supply ratios by center type are shown in Table 13.

The parking supply ratios were also calculated for each center size. Centers with 400,000 to 599,999 square feet provided the highest average number of parking spaces per 1,000 square feet, with 5.5. Conversely, centers between 1,500,000 and 2,500,000 square feet offered the lowest average number of spaces per 1,000 square feet, with 4.6. Parking supply ratios by center size are shown in Table 14.

In conclusion, the parking supply is higher than the parking demand by an average of almost a full space per 1,000 square feet of GLA for centers smaller than 600,000 square feet, and by about half a space for larger centers. This suggests that the parking supply is not constricting demand. Moreover, it suggests that building more parking spaces will not result in increased traffic volumes and, subsequently, in increased sales at centers.

Table 13
Parking Supply Ratios by Center Type

Center Type	Number of Centers Responding	Parking Ratio (Parking Spaces per 1,000 Square Feet of Occupied GLA)			
		Low	Average	High	Standard Deviation
Neighborhood	121	1.4	4.9	8.6	1.2
Community	104	0.6	4.7	11.7	1.4
Regional	69	2.2	5.3	7.3	1.0
Super Regional	97	3.4	5.0	6.4	0.5
Fashion/Specialty	7	4.6	5.3	6.0	0.5
Power	23	2.4	5.2	7.4	1.2
Theme/Entertainment	15	3.0	5.9	12.1	2.0
Outlet	8	3.4	5.4	8.9	1.8
Other	6	3.1	4.6	6.6	1.6
Total	**450**				

Table 14
Parking Supply Ratios by Center Size

Center Size (GLA in Square Feet)	Number of Responses	Parking Ratio (Parking Spaces per 1,000 Square Feet of Occupied GLA)			
		Low	Average	High	Standard Deviation
Less than 400,000	286	0.6	4.9	11.7	1.3
400,000–599,999	37	3.3	5.5	12.1	1.5
600,000–1,499,999	141	2.7	5.1	7.3	0.7
1,500,000–2,500,000	11	4.1	4.6	5.1	0.3
Total	**475**				

Fifteen different shopping centers were selected as case studies. The selected centers completed a questionnaire regarding their size, transit service (if applicable), surrounding land use, tenant classifications, and parking conditions. Each participating center was chosen based on regional location, center type, and owner/managing company. Consequently, the distribution of shopping centers in the case studies reflects the diversity of centers in the full study.

While the level of parking demand was not a factor in selecting the case studies, it was discovered that eight of the 15 case study centers experienced parking demand higher than the recommended ratios. Thus, they offer some practical examples of coping with higher-than-expected parking demands, a happy circumstance if it translates into more business. For two of these eight centers, the peak demand found during the survey period was slightly higher than the rec-

ommended ratios, but statistically virtually the same. For three of the eight centers, the data collection time period— 1:00 p.m. to 3:00 p.m. on December 12, 1998—was busier than the 20th busiest hour. (It was possible to discover this since these centers also had continuous counting programs.)

Shady Brook Mall

The Shady Brook Mall is a small, enclosed community center in the historic city of Columbia, Tennessee, population 32,043. Columbia is situated approximately 45 miles south of Nashville in the heart of Maury County. Tourist attractions include former U.S. president James K. Polk's ancestral home. Every year during the first week in April, the Mule Day Parade attracts nearly 200,000 spectators and generates increased activity at the Shady Brook Mall.

The total site area of the Shady Brook Mall is 1,324,660 square feet. Four major tenants occupy about 62 percent of the center's 282,272 square feet of GLA: Sears (63,156 square feet), JC Penney (51,324 square feet), Peeble's (38,010 square feet), and Goody's (22,500 square feet). There is no office space or restaurant service within the premises, and no cinema is present on the immediate grounds. However, an 11-plex cinema is in very close proximity, and it does occasionally affect parking demand at the mall even though it has no direct relation to the mall. The surrounding land use is commercial.

The site is anchored at the corner of Lawrence Street and the Columbia Bypass. The center's 1,558 parking spaces provide a parking supply of 6.3 spaces per 1,000 square feet of occupied GLA. There were 1,556 parked cars during the survey day, yielding a parking demand of 6.3 parked cars per 1,000 occupied square feet. There is no transit service to the center.

Interior View: Goody's

Interior View: JCPenney

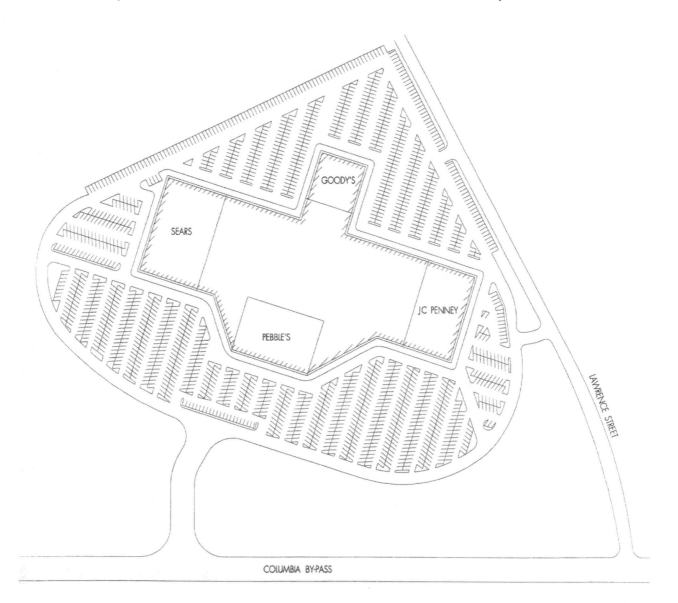

Carousel Center

The Carousel Center, a super regional center just north of downtown Syracuse, New York, is one of the largest centers examined in this study. Its urban setting has undergone major redevelopment since 1988. The redevelopment area covers more than 800 acres in the downtown and surrounding areas. More than $1.5 billion in public and private funding has transformed Syracuse, previously known as the "Oil City," into one of the most dynamic redevelopment areas in the country. The parking and transportation needs of the Carousel Center have been significantly affected.

The center is surrounded on the northwest and southwest by Onondaga Lake. Interstate 81 provides an anchor along the northeast boundary. Hiawatha Boulevard runs along the southeast border. The Carousel Center has a total site area of about 77 acres. Major tenants include JC Penney, Lord & Taylor, Kaufmann's,

Carousel Center

Aerial View

Bon-Ton, Bonwit Teller, Best Buy, and Hills. These major tenants occupy slightly less than half of the 1,531,972 square feet of GLA. Additional tenants include a 19-plex cinema (76,000 square feet) and 18 restaurants (63,489 total square feet). Only 50,732 square feet are vacant. The surrounding land use is commercial.

The Carousel Center has a parking supply of 7,172 spaces, yielding a parking supply ratio of 4.7 spaces per 1,000 occupied square feet. Parking during the survey day generated a demand of 4.7 parked cars per 1,000 square feet of occupied GLA. To diminish the demand for parking, the center strongly promotes the Centro Bus Stop transit service to its patrons and offers the On-Track Rail Platform.

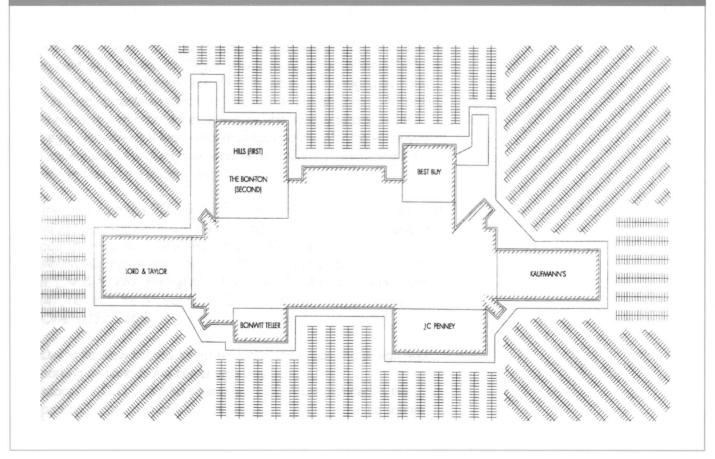

The Showcase

The Showcase is a theme/entertainment center on the lower Las Vegas Strip, directly in front of the MGM Grand Hotel and Theme Park. With its ostentatious appearance, select major tenants, and location in the heart of the city, the Showcase is marketed almost entirely as a tourist attraction. It is managed by Forest City. According to managing officials at the Showcase, there is less tourist activity during the holiday season in Las Vegas than during the rest of the year. Consequently, during the survey day of the study, parking demand at the Showcase was much less than normal.

The Showcase has 200,366 square feet of GLA. Only 2,358 square feet were left vacant at the time of this study. Casinos, restaurants, and retail stores surround the center. All of the occupied GLA is maintained by five major tenants: the World of Coca-Cola (33,563 square feet), M & M World/Ethel M. Chocolates (28,486 square feet), GameWorks (47,161 square feet), the All Star Café (36,172 square feet), and United Artists Cinema (52,226 square feet).

Due to the slowness of the tourist season in Las Vegas during the holidays, the design-hour parking demand at this center was very light. Over 7.2 spaces per 1,000 square feet of occupied GLA are included in the parking supply, and only 2.1 parked cars per 1,000 square feet of occupied GLA were observed on the survey day. The entire parking supply is located in a parking structure. A flat rate of $2 per day is charged for parking. According to management, adequate parking is available at the Showcase on all but one day of the year. There is no transit service to this center.

East Wing

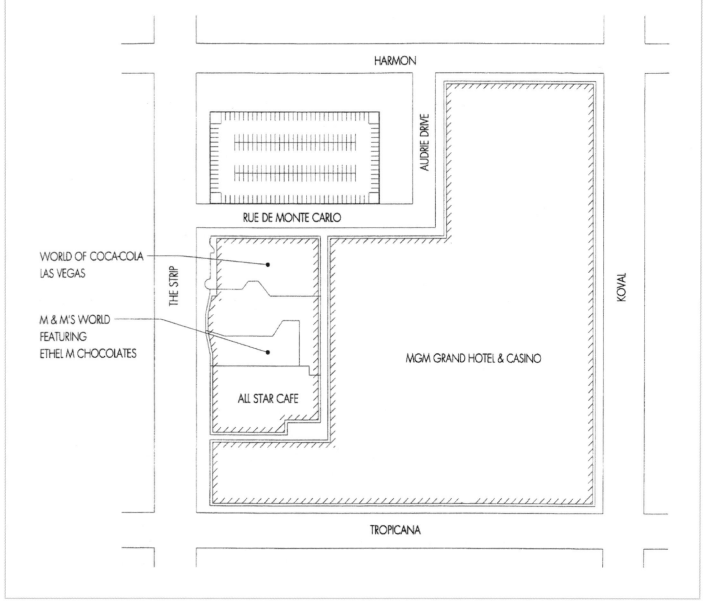

Camelback Colonnade

The Camelback Colonnade, managed by the Westcor Company, was developed in several phases beginning in 1963. Designed as an enclosed mall, it was partially demolished and renovated in 1994 and 1995, resulting in an open-air power center with about 15,000 square feet of enclosed common area. This center has some second-level office space leased to a major telecommunications company, 12 anchor tenants, and a ministorage warehouse in the basement.

The Camelback Colonnade is situated at the southwest corner of 20th Street and Camelback Road in Phoenix, Arizona. The center also has substantial frontage on Highland Avenue. Access at the south entrance is provided by an off-ramp from the Squaw Peak Parkway along Highland Avenue.

Camelback Colonnade

Aerial View

The total site area is 1,785,731 square feet, and the total occupied GLA is 607,078 square feet. Approximately 22,346 square feet are left vacant. Mervyn's, Smith's, Best Buy, and Last Chance are the four largest tenants, occupying over 38 percent of the total GLA. Other major tenants include Marshall's, Linens Plus, Michael's, Old Navy, and Staples. Office space and restaurant service constitute over 18 percent of the total GLA. The size of the property is typical for the area, and there are no known factors to prevent the site from development to its highest and best use.

The land surrounding the Camelback Colonnade includes retail, hotel, office, and theater space. Transit service is provided by the Valley Metro. The parking supply is 2,875 total spaces, which yields a parking supply ratio of 4.3 spaces per 1,000 square feet of occupied GLA. During the survey day, there were 3.3 parked cars per 1,000 square feet of occupied GLA.

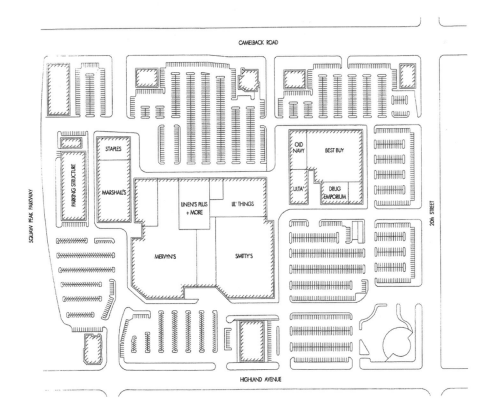

Village Fair

Village Fair, a power center in Phoenix, Arizona, opened in October 1990. This center, also managed by the Westcor Company, is quite similar to the Camelback Colonnade, although it is only one-third its size. Anchors are provided by Toys "R" Us, Sports Authority, and Best Buy. Best Buy owns its own parcel and is not included as a major tenant. Minor anchors include Ultra 3, Bookstar, Office Max, and Linens Plus.

Village Fair is located southwest of the corner of Tatum Boulevard and Paradise Village Parkway East. Exclusive of the ground leased buildings, there are 16 existing tenant suites ranging from 620 to 39,238 square feet in size, and the existing bay depths range between 25 and 100 feet. The total site area is 1,066,823 square feet, and the total occupied GLA is 209,030 square feet. There is no vacant space.

Currently, retail shops, golf, cinema, hotel, and office space surround Village Fair. Restaurants at the center occupy 11,000 square feet. Of the total occupied GLA, Toys "R" Us and Sports Authority account for over 40 percent and the minor anchors (Ultra 3, Bookstar, Office Max, and Linens Plus) for slightly under 28 percent. Village Fair has no office space or theater.

Parking conditions at Village Fair are adequate. The parking supply is 1,266 spaces, which yields 6.4 parked cars per 1,000 square feet of occupied GLA, and on the survey day there were 5.2 parked cars per 1,000 square feet of occupied GLA. Transit service is available via Phoenix Transit, but it does not enter the center property. Instead, a scheduled bus service exists at a shopping center directly across the street. Management at Village Fair indicated that parking is fully occupied (over 95 percent) approximately three days per year.

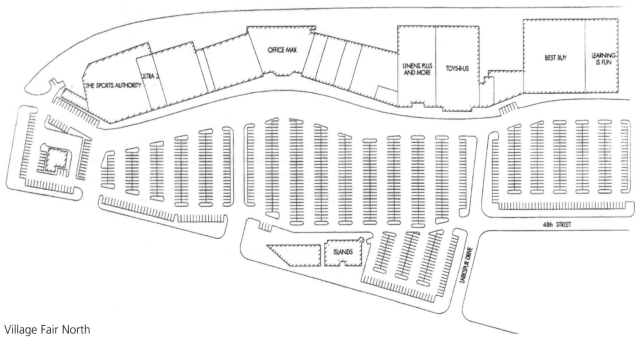

Village Fair North

Plaza Frontenac

Located in Saint Louis, Missouri, Plaza Frontenac is an upscale shopping center that houses many specialty shops and premier stores. It is classified as a fashion/specialty center. Heitman Retail manages the property, which is positioned in a large urban setting.

Plaza Frontenac has 48 stores and shops, including two anchor tenants. The total site area is 714,063 square feet, with 443,750 square feet of gross leasable area. There are 12,067 square feet left vacant. Saks Fifth Avenue and Neiman Marcus, the major tenants, occupy approximately 59 percent of the total GLA. Restaurants, all non-fast-food, occupy 21,387 square feet. A six-plex cinema occupies 3.2 percent of the GLA. Of the remaining 45 tenants, 19 are clothing stores.

Plaza Frontenac has adequate parking throughout each day of the year. Even during the holiday shopping season, its parking facilities are never fully occupied. Of its 2,200 parking spaces, 1,880 are located in surface lots. The remaining 220 spaces are located in a two-level parking structure. Patrons and employees are never charged for parking. However, employees are required to park in designated areas away from the building in order to provide more convenient parking for customers.

To maintain adequate parking, the center participates in its local Transportation Management Association and provides bus service onto the property. This center has a parking supply of 5.0 parking spaces per 1,000 square feet of occupied GLA. The conditions during the survey day generated 4.0 parked cars per 1,000 square feet of occupied GLA.

Plaza Frontenac

North Wing, Aerial View

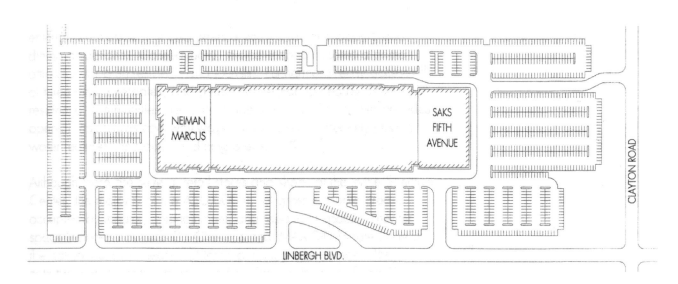

NEIMAN MARCUS

SAKS FIFTH AVENUE

CLAYTON ROAD

LINBERGH BLVD.

Irvine Spectrum Center

Originally opened in 1995, the Irvine Spectrum Center is a premiere entertainment center located in southern California. In addition to entertainment, it offers a wide array of shopping and dining attractions. Consequently, this center has become a prime attraction for both residents and tourists. Easy access off three main interstates and a tight connection to nearby affluent residential communities make its setting ideal. Open-air courtyards and walkways contain specialty paving, water features, and outdoor dining areas.

Although there are several retail stores and shops at the Irvine Spectrum Center, most of the 450,000 square feet of gross leasable area is occupied by theaters, entertainment tenants, and restaurants. The theaters include Edwards 21 Cinemas and IMAX 3-D Theater, one of the nation's busiest theaters in terms of annual attendance. The entertainment tenants are anchored by Dave & Buster's, Sega City,

Irvine Spectrum Center

and NASCAR Silicon Motor Speedway. In addition to its vast selection of non-fast-food restaurants, the center features a ten-restaurant, 300-seat restaurant court.

The parking conditions at the Irvine Spectrum Center are changing. The center is executing a major expansion project, which will almost double the total GLA when completed. However, the parking lots have already been expanded, and an immense excess of parking spaces now exists. (The parking ratio currently is 12.1 spaces per 1,000 square feet of occupied GLA.) Once the current phase of construction is completed, the parking ratio will be much more balanced. During the survey day, the parking ratio was 3.6 parked cars per 1,000 square feet of occupied GLA, indicating that the parking supply is adequate. Transit service, provided by the Transportation Corridor, gives direct access from all of Orange County to the Irvine Spectrum Center.

Lakepointe Crossing

Lakepointe Crossing is located in Lewisville, Texas, approximately 20 miles northwest of downtown Dallas. This suburban super regional center contains 588,732 square feet, 48,098 square feet of which is outparcel space. All of the GLA currently is occupied.

The parking supply at this center provides 3,554 spaces. There is no parking structure, and customers and employees are not charged for parking. Based on the judgment of the management, the parking lots are fully occupied at least ten times per year. All of these days occur during the month of December and occupancy reflects normal seasonal/holiday activity.

Lakepointe Crossing

Aerial View

Even with the busy seasonal activity, parking conditions, according to management, are adequate. Unauthorized parking is not a problem, and the surrounding land use does not generate parking on the shopping center's property. Employees use the parking lots behind the building during peak shopping periods to provide adequate parking for customers. Lakepointe Crossing has a parking supply of 6.6 spaces per 1,000 square feet of occupied GLA. The conditions during the survey day generated 5.6 parked cars per 1,000 square feet of occupied GLA.

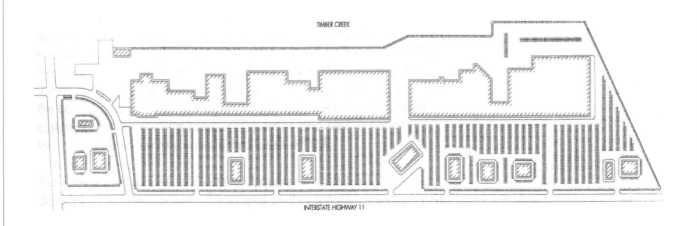

Castleton Square

Castleton Square is a super regional center managed by the Simon Property Group. Located approximately 12 miles northeast of downtown Indianapolis, Indiana, it is easily accessible off of Interstate 465 and 82nd Street. The center, which opened in 1973, was renovated in November 1998. Although the renovations have greatly enhanced the appeal of the center to its patrons, orienting customers to the new ring road configuration and new entrance locations has been difficult.

The total occupied GLA of Castleton Square is 1,384,527 square feet, and 36,934 square feet remain vacant. The largest anchor tenant is Lazarus, with 309,080 square feet. The other anchors—Sears, L.S. Ayres, Galyan's, JC Penney, and Von Maur—account for approximately 75 percent of the center's total occupied GLA. In addition, the center has 17,500 square feet of restaurant space and 11,833 square feet devoted to a theater. The remaining tenants are 112 specialty shops, which together occupy 316,500 square feet.

Castleton Square has a total supply of 7,606 parking spaces. Included in the supply is a two-level, 256-space parking structure where customers can park without charge. A recent parking count determined that on-site parking is fully occupied three days per year: the Friday after Thanksgiving, and the two Saturdays immediately preceding Christmas Day. Management stated that the greatest parking challenge is urging customers to use the reconfigured parking areas on what was once the "back" side of the mall. During the survey day, Castleton Square had a parking demand of 5.2 parked cars per 1,000 square feet of GLA. The current parking supply is 5.4 parking spaces per 1,000 square feet of GLA.

Aerial View

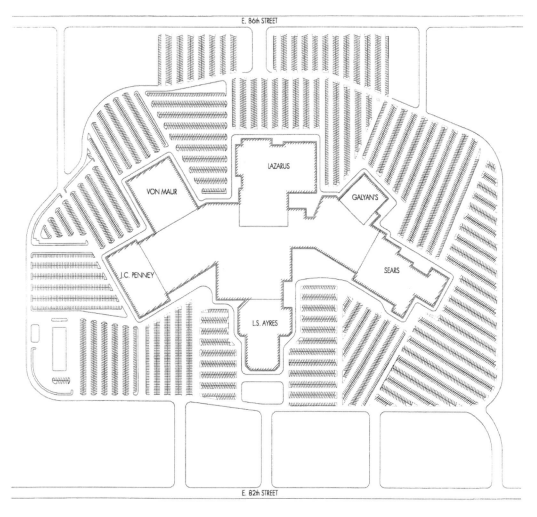

Plaza Del Sol

The Plaza Del Sol Mall is a small community center located in Del Rio, Texas. It is one of the few centers participating in the study that is in a rural or highway nonsuburban setting. The city of Del Rio is immediately across the international border of Ciudad Acuna, Mexico. Lake Amistad in Del Rio helps generate activity at the center due to hunting, fishing, and water sports. Managed by CBL and Associates Management, Inc., Plaza Del Sol is the only shopping center in Del Rio.

Plaza Del Sol has 260,242 square feet of gross leasable area. Approximately 5 percent of the area is vacant, and the remaining 95 percent is currently leased to 39 tenants. The anchor tenants are provided by Kmart, Bealls, and JC Penney. Kmart is the largest anchor with 87,461 square feet, nearly 34 percent of the Plaza Del Sol's total GLA. Bealls has 30,000 square feet and JC Penney has 38,720

Plaza Del Sol

Aerial Views

square feet. Other tenants occupy 790 square feet of office space and 9,470 square feet of non-fast-food restaurant space. Plaza Del Sol also has an eight-screen, 24,814-square-foot movie theater.

The management of this center conducted recent parking occupancy counts and found that the parking lots were fully occupied approximately five times per year: Christmas Eve, the weekend prior to Christmas, Easter weekend, Halloween, and during an annual car stereo show. The total number of parking spaces on site is 1,340, all of which are located in surface lots. Employees can park in the surface lots, although they are required to park along the outer perimeters of the lots. Plaza Del Sol has implemented a bus service for its transit patrons. The parking supply is 5.0 spaces per 1,000 square feet of occupied GLA. There were 4.8 parked cars per 1,000 square feet of occupied GLA during the survey day.

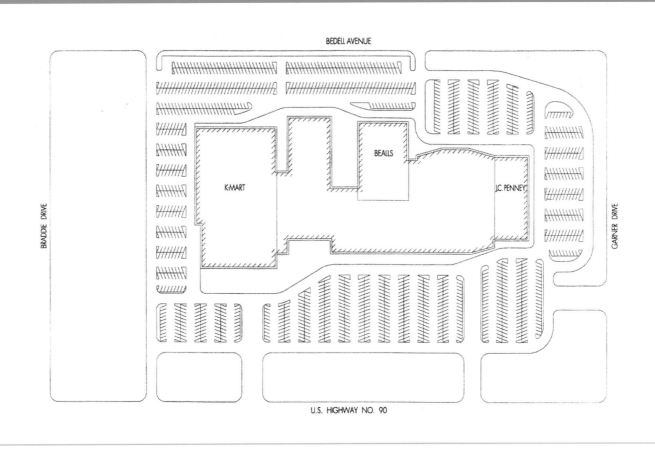

Chapel Hills Mall

Located on the northern outskirts of Colorado Springs, Colorado, Chapel Hills Mall is a large, super regional shopping center. Although near a large city, the center is far enough from Colorado Springs to be considered in a suburban setting. The economy in the Colorado Springs area has thrived throughout the past decade. Consequently, employment rates have increased, which has led to a population increase. Moreover, shopping center vacancies have declined, and construction of retail space has been steadily on the rise. These trends are expected to continue.

The total site area at the Chapel Hills Mall is 99.93 acres, and the gross leasable area is 1,206,334 square feet. There are 33,598 square feet of vacant space. The major tenants occupy approximately 62 percent of the total GLA. They are JC Penney (62,422 square feet), Foley's (171,083 square feet), Sears (132,369 square feet), Dillard's (207,141 square feet), Mervyn's (82,499 square feet), and Kmart (27,977 square feet). Restaurants occupy 19,800 square feet and cinemas 49,586 square feet. Altogether, the Chapel Hills Mall has 122 tenants.

A parking structure at Chapel Hills Mall provides approximately 10 percent of its total parking supply. Although management at the center indicated that expansion of the parking area was unnecessary, it did state that parking was fully occupied ten or more days per year. Like virtually every center surveyed, parking at capacity at Chapel Hills Mall occurs during the holiday season. At this time, employees are required to park on the outer perimeters of the parking lots. The parking supply at this center is 5.0 spaces per 1,000 square feet of occupied GLA, and there were 4.8 parked cars per 1,000 square feet of occupied GLA during the survey day.

Chapel Hills Mall

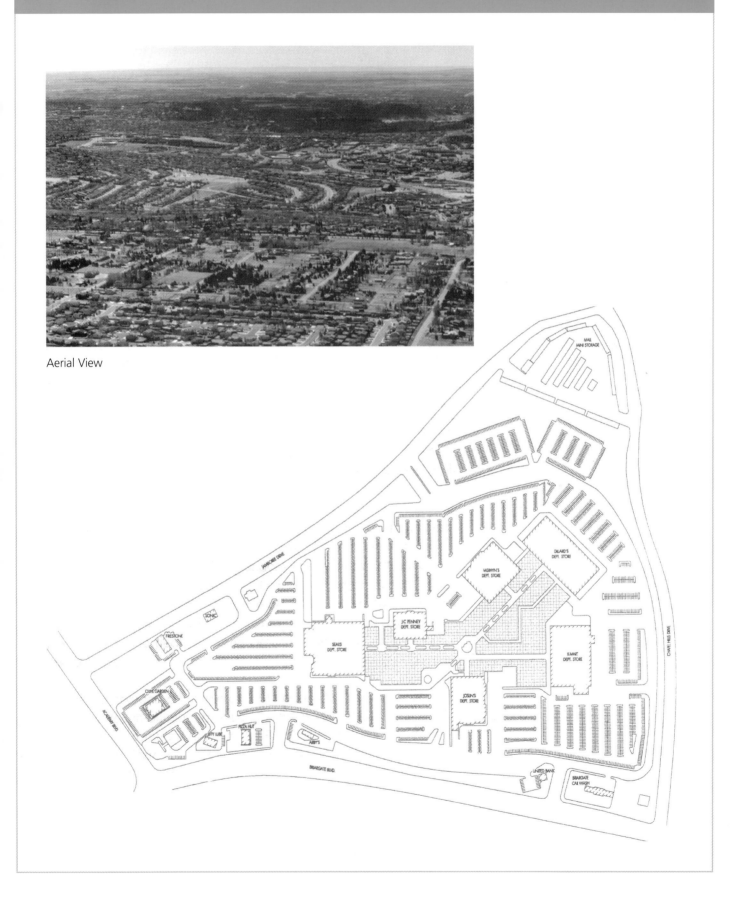

Aerial View

Santa Monica Place

Santa Monica Place, a subsidiary of the Rouse Company, is a three-level regional center located in Santa Monica, California. Because of its southern California location, it has been included in scenes from several Hollywood blockbuster films. Furthermore, the close proximity of Santa Monica Pier and beach provides a historic setting for this center, which was constructed in 1980. It is located on the south end of Third Street Promenade, at the intersection of Fourth and Broadway.

Santa Monica Place has approximately 570,000 square feet and accommodates 140 tenants. Two anchor tenants, Robinsons-May and Macy's, are positioned diagonally to each other, and they are both adjacent to a parking structure.

According to management, enforcing parking and controlling access to the center's two parking structures is a difficult task. There are 2,020 parking spaces within the two structures, yielding a parking supply of 3.5 spaces per 1,000 square feet of occupied GLA. Demand during the survey day generated 4.0 parked cars per 1,000 square feet of occupied GLA. Therefore, employees are required to park off site during peak shopping periods in order to provide adequate parking for customers.

Patrons are charged a flat rate of $3 to park after 5:00 p.m. on Thursday through Sunday, although the fee is waived with a minimum $25 purchase at the mall. Parking at all other times is for three hours. Management has indicated that capacity parking exists more than ten times per year, mainly on Saturday afternoons. Public transportation is provided by the Santa Monica Big Blue Bus and by Greyhound. Employees who use public transportation are reimbursed by the center.

Main Entrance

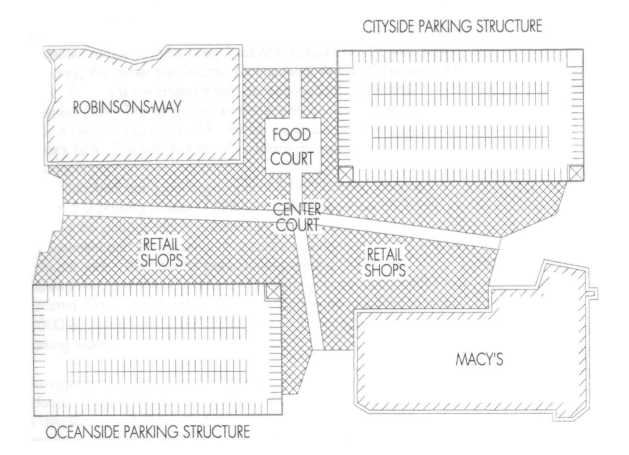

Cielo Vista Mall

Cielo Vista Mall is a large, super regional shopping center located in El Paso, Texas. This 1,167,140-square-foot center is managed by the Simon Property Group. The total site area encompasses 83 acres.

Cielo Vista Mall has 123 stores. Dillard's is the largest tenant, occupying 26 percent of the total occupied GLA. The remaining anchor tenants—Montgomery Ward, JC Penney, and Sears—occupy 42 percent, and restaurants occupy 2 percent. This mall has no office space or cinema.

Cielo Vista Mall has a parking supply of 6,000 spaces, yielding a ratio of 5.2 parking spaces per 1,000 square feet of occupied GLA. None of the parking supply is contained within a structure, and management said parking is at its capacity approximately four to six times per year. Peak parking days are the Friday after Thanksgiving and the Saturdays and weekdays immediately before Christmas Day. During the survey day, the number of parked cars per 1,000 square feet of occupied GLA was 5.3, slightly higher than the parking supply.

Management at Cielo Vista Mall has taken several steps to maintain adequate parking conditions. Employees are required to park in remote areas at all times. During the holiday season, employees must park even farther away from the store entrances. Warning tickets or stickers are placed on vehicles parked in unauthorized areas, and the local police department often assists in the ticketing procedure.

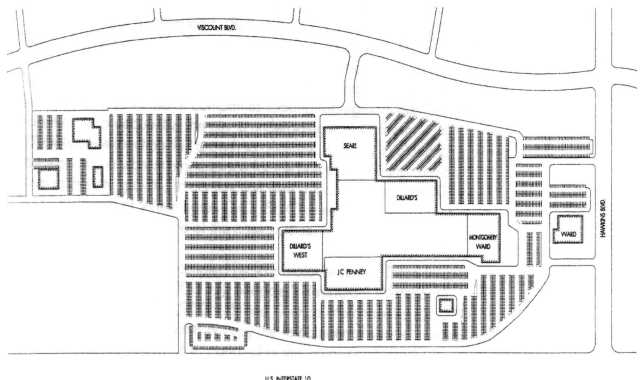

St. Charles Towne Plaza

St. Charles Towne Plaza is a community center located in the suburban setting of Waldorf, Maryland, less than 40 miles southeast of Washington, D.C. Built in 1987, it is managed by the Simon Property Group. The city of Waldorf is located on the periphery of the Washington, D.C.–Baltimore metropolitan area, the fourth largest consumer market in the United States, making it attractive to businesses of all sizes. Moreover, its remarkably large industrial zone has drawn the attention of several major companies looking for regional distribution facilities. Consequently, the city is undergoing rapid growth. City officials expect this growth to continue, and they have high hopes that Waldorf will develop into a vibrant marketplace for the entire Mid-Atlantic region.

The major part of the GLA is occupied by four major tenants. These tenants include Hechinger (70,000 square feet), Shopper's Restaurant Warehouse (94,028 square feet), Ames (78,900 square feet), and Service Merchandise (51,250 square feet). In addition, 25 tenants occupy the remainder of space. Overall, the total GLA is 403,212 square feet, and all of the area is occupied.

St. Charles Towne Plaza does occasionally lack adequate parking for its employees and patrons. According to its management, parking is fully occupied more than ten days per year. As a means of solving some of the parking problems, employees are required to park along the outer periphery of the parking lots. However, no incentive is offered to employees to encourage carpooling, and the center does not have a transit system. St. Charles Towne Plaza has a parking supply of 5.8 spaces per 1,000 square feet of occupied GLA. The parking occupancy counts indicated a ratio of 4.4 parked cars per 1,000 square feet of occupied GLA during the survey day.

Shopper's Food Warehouse Entrance

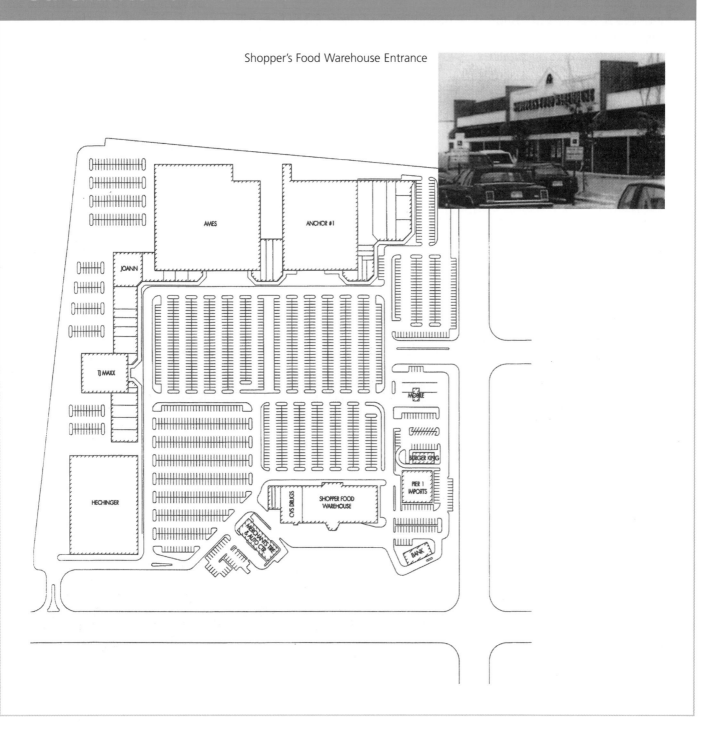

Independence Mall

Independence Mall, located a few miles west of Cape Cod Bay, is approximately 30 miles southeast of Boston, Massachusetts. It is a regional center managed by the Pyramid Management Group.

The total GLA of the center is 751,768 square feet; 77,000 square feet currently are vacant. The center is anchored by Filene's, Bradlees, JC Penney, and Sears; these tenants occupy approximately 50 percent of the total GLA. In addition, the center has offices, a 14-screen movie cinema, restaurant service, and almost 100 specialty shops.

The parking supply of 3,956 spaces is in surface lots. According to management, full capacity parking usually is reached between four and six times a year due to seasonal peak activity combined

Independence Mall

Aerial View

with a special event. There are no restrictions regarding employee parking except during the holiday shopping season, when employees must park at least 20 spaces away from the building. Parking demand during the survey day generated a need for 3,265 spaces; the ratio was 4.2 parked cars per 1,000 square feet of occupied GLA. The parking supply yields a ratio of 5.1 parked cars per 1,000 square feet of occupied GLA.

The management at Independence Mall has not indicated any need for major improvements in the current parking system. The only problems related to parking are caused by snowstorms, when patrons tend to triple-park, and by the small number of parking spaces near entrances and destination shops.

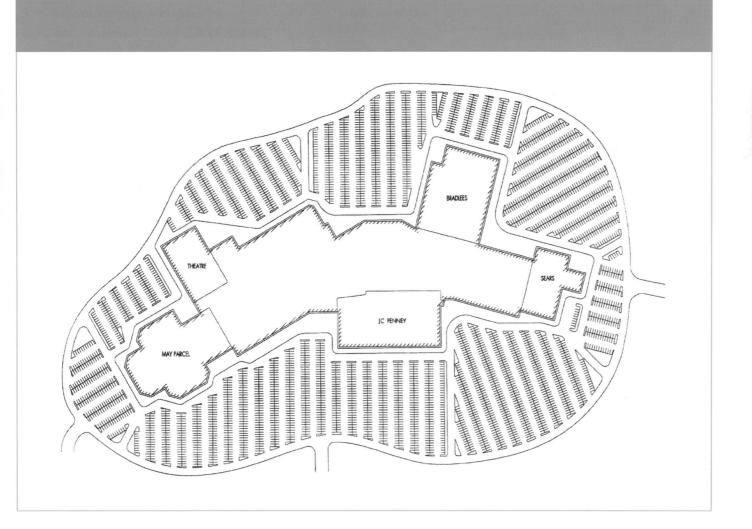

Appendices

Appendix A
Recommended Parking Ratios[a]

Percentage of Total GLA in Combined Cinema, Restaurant, and Entertainment Usages

Center Size (GLA in Square Feet)	0%	1%	2%	3%	4%	5%	6%	7%	8%	9%	10%	11%	12%	13%	14%	15%	16%	17%	18%	19%	20%	21%+
0–400,000	4.00	4.00	4.00	4.00	4.00	4.00	4.00	4.00	4.00	4.00	4.00	4.03	4.06	4.09	4.12	4.15	4.18	4.21	4.24	4.27	4.30	SP[b]
400,000–419,999	4.00	4.00	4.00	4.00	4.00	4.00	4.00	4.00	4.00	4.00	4.00	4.03	4.06	4.09	4.12	4.15	4.18	4.21	4.24	4.27	4.30	SP[b]
420,000–439,999	4.06	4.06	4.06	4.06	4.06	4.06	4.06	4.06	4.06	4.06	4.06	4.09	4.12	4.15	4.18	4.21	4.24	4.27	4.30	4.33	4.36	SP[b]
440,000–459,999	4.11	4.11	4.11	4.11	4.11	4.11	4.11	4.11	4.11	4.11	4.11	4.14	4.17	4.20	4.23	4.26	4.29	4.32	4.35	4.38	4.41	SP[b]
460,000–479,999	4.17	4.17	4.17	4.17	4.17	4.17	4.17	4.17	4.17	4.17	4.17	4.20	4.23	4.26	4.29	4.32	4.35	4.38	4.41	4.44	4.47	SP[b]
480,000–499,999	4.22	4.22	4.22	4.22	4.22	4.22	4.22	4.22	4.22	4.22	4.22	4.25	4.28	4.31	4.34	4.37	4.40	4.43	4.46	4.49	4.52	SP[b]
500,000–519,999	4.28	4.28	4.28	4.28	4.28	4.28	4.28	4.28	4.28	4.28	4.28	4.31	4.34	4.37	4.40	4.43	4.46	4.49	4.52	4.55	4.58	SP[b]
520,000–539,999	4.33	4.33	4.33	4.33	4.33	4.33	4.33	4.33	4.33	4.33	4.33	4.36	4.39	4.42	4.45	4.48	4.51	4.54	4.57	4.60	4.63	SP[b]
540,000–559,999	4.39	4.39	4.39	4.39	4.39	4.39	4.39	4.39	4.39	4.39	4.39	4.42	4.45	4.48	4.51	4.54	4.57	4.60	4.63	4.66	4.69	SP[b]
560,000–579,999	4.44	4.44	4.44	4.44	4.44	4.44	4.44	4.44	4.44	4.44	4.44	4.47	4.50	4.53	4.56	4.59	4.62	4.65	4.68	4.71	4.74	SP[b]
580,000–599,999	4.50	4.50	4.50	4.50	4.50	4.50	4.50	4.50	4.50	4.50	4.50	4.53	4.56	4.59	4.62	4.65	4.68	4.71	4.74	4.77	4.80	SP[b]
600,000–2,500,00	4.50	4.50	4.50	4.50	4.50	4.50	4.50	4.50	4.50	4.50	4.50	4.53	4.56	4.59	4.62	4.65	4.68	4.71	4.74	4.77	4.80	SP[b]

a   Parked cars per 1,000 square feet of gross leasable area.

b   Shared parking methology is recommended. Shared parking is defined as parking spaces that can be used to serve two or more individual land uses without conflict or encroachment.

Dear Center Manager:

Greetings and best regards for the upcoming holiday season to you and your family.

Walker Parking Consultants (WPC) has been retained by the Urban Land Institute (ULI) and the International Council of Shopping Centers (ICSC) to survey shopping center parking. This information will be used to update the landmark ULI/ICSC study (in 1982), which became the primary source of guidance on parking requirements and benchmarks for the shopping center industry. The retail environment has changed significantly during the past 15 years, and the original study is very much in need of an update. Your assistance in accomplishing that update could not be more important.

There are two ways by which you can assist our industry through your participation in this study:

The first is to fill out the enclosed questionnaire and return it to our study consultant Walker Parking Consultants. The survey form is designed in a multiple choice format and should require about ten minutes to complete.

The second is to assist in on-site data collection in your parking lot during peak shopping days next year. Details are spelled out at the end of the survey form.

The information obtained will be kept confidential and will only be used collectively.

If you have any questions or need assistance in completing this form, please contact John Dorsett with Walker Parking Consultants at 1-317-842-6890.

Looking forward to working with you, we are...

John Konarski III, Ph.D.
Staff Vice President
International Council of Shopping Centers

Rachelle L. Levitt
Senior Vice President, Policy and Practice
Urban Land Institute

To Be Completed by Center Management

Name of Center: _____
(Please indicate only one center per form. If additional forms are needed, please photocopy or request additional forms from WPC.)

Address of this Center: _____

_____

_____

Contact Person: _____

Title: _____

Telephone: (_____) _____

Address (if different from above): _____

_____

_____

Information for This Center:

A. Shopping center location (check one box and insert ZIP Code)
   ❏ Urban setting in a large city (over 250,000 people)
   ❏ Urban setting in a town, suburban business district or edge city
   ❏ Suburban location
   ❏ Rural or highway non-suburban location

   ❏ Other: (Describe) _____

B. ZIP Code in which center is physically located: _____

C. Type of shopping center (Refer to enclosed definition sheet and check only one)
   ❏ Neighborhood center
   ❏ Community center
   ❏ Regional center
   ❏ Super regional center
   ❏ Fashion/specialty center
   ❏ Power center
   ❏ Theme/entertainment center
   ❏ Factory Outlet center
   ❏ Other (Describe)_____

D. Vacancy and Occupancy as of December 1998: (**Occupied** space refers to space *physically occupied* by tenants, whether owned or unowned, and includes temporary tenants and anchors. **Vacant** space refers to spaces designated for occupancy that are *not physically occupied* by tenants, anchors or temporary tenants, even if currently leased. Occupied and vacant space square footage should be as of **December 1998.** If there has been a significant change in occupancy during December, provide averages for the month.)

   1. Total occupied gross leasable area excluding outparcels (include anchors, whether owned or unowned, and temporary tenants) _____ square feet

   2. Total occupied outparcel space, including anchors and temporary tenants, that functions as part of the center (whether owned or unowned) _____ square feet

   3. Total vacant gross leasable area (including anchor and outparcel space, whether owned or unowned) _____ square feet

E. Tenant mix characteristics

   This center (including owned or unowned outparcel space that functions as part of the center) has:

   Movie theater space:
   Occupied _____ square feet   Vacant _____ square feet
   Total seats _____   Total screens _____

   Non-movie theater commercial recreation space (bowling alley, skating rink, health club, arcade, virtual reality venue, etc.) _____ square feet

   Fast-food space (including food court seating area) _____ square feet

   Non-fast-food restaurant space _____ square feet

   Grocery/supermarket space _____ square feet

   Discount/off-price store space _____ square feet

   Office tenant space:
   Occupied _____ square feet   Vacant _____ square feet

   Other non-retail space (bank branch, library, day care, post office, tax preparation, travel agency, etc.) _____ square feet

Parking at This Center:

A. Total number of parking spaces on site: _____

B. Are any of these spaces in a parking garage, deck, or other structure? ❏ No   ❏ Yes

    If yes, how many spaces are in a garage or structure? _____

    What is the highest vertical garage level? _____

C. Is there any parking charge to the customer?
   ❏ No   ❏ Yes

    If yes, what is the initial rate? $_____ for _____ hours

    What is the subsequent rate? $_____ for _____ hours

    Is there a parking validation program (by stores/tenants)?
    ❏ No   ❏ Yes

       If yes, describe: _____

    _____

    Is there a valet parking program at this center?
    ❏ No   ❏ Yes

D. How many days per year is on-site parking fully occupied (over 95%) at any time during the day?

    ❏ Never   ❏ Four to six

    ❏ One   ❏ Seven to nine

    ❏ Two   ❏ Ten or more

    ❏ Three

    Additional comments: _____

    _____

       This answer is based on:

       ❏ Recent count   ❏   Judgment/past experience

E. When is on-site parking fully occupied? _____

    _____
    (Please provide specific dates or times, for example, Friday after Thanksgiving, Saturday before Christmas, every Friday evening, Saturday afternoons, etc.)

F. Is peak parking demand at this center usually associated with:

    ❏ A special event or promotion?

    ❏ Normal seasonal/holiday activity?

    ❏ A combination of seasonal peak with a special event?

G. Does this shopping center participate in a local or regional Transportation Management Association? ❏ No   ❏ Yes

H. Do shopping center tenant employees park on site during off-peak seasons? ❏ No   ❏ Yes

    Where do the tenant employees park? _____

    _____

    If they park on site, are specific spaces reserved for employees?
    ❏ No   ❏ Yes

       If yes, where are those spaces located? _____

    _____

       If yes, how many spaces are reserved? _____

    Are employees ever charged for parking? ❏ No   ❏ Yes

    Are incentives provided to encourage employees to carpool or use transit (such as carpool matching or subsidized bus passes)?
    ❏ No   ❏ Yes

       If yes, describe: _____

    _____

    Please estimate the number of employees (both retailer and center) working in the center during:

    Normal period _____   Peak period _____

    Are shopping center employees asked to park in a different location during peak shopping times? ❏ No   ❏ Yes

       If yes, describe: _____

    _____

I. How many handicapped parking spaces are provided? _____

    Is violation of handicapped parking a common occurrence at your center? ❏ No   ❏ Yes

J. Are there spaces designated for compact cars?
    ❏ No   ❏ Yes

       If yes, how many? _____

K. Do parkers from adjacent properties or land uses frequently park on shopping center property? ❏ No   ❏ Yes

       If yes, 1. Describe: _____

               _____

             2. Does this have a significant effect on parking availability for your shoppers? ❏ No   ❏ Yes

If yes, describe: _____

_____

3. Has any action been taken to curb unauthorized parking? ❏ No   ❏ Yes

If yes, describe: _____

L. What are your three biggest parking-related problems? (Please rank in descending order of significance.)

1. _____

_____

2. _____

_____

3. _____

_____

M. Has there been any need to increase parking area, since the center opened, that was not associated with an expansion of tenant floor area? ❏ No   ❏ Yes

N. Please use this space to provide any further thoughts you may have on parking availability, management, or utilization.

_____

_____

_____

_____

TRANSIT AT THIS CENTER

A. Is there scheduled bus or train service to the shopping center area? ❏ No   ❏ Yes, bus   ❏ Yes, train

B. Do buses enter the center property?   ❏ No   ❏ Yes

C. Which of the following amenities are provided for transit patrons? ❏ No   ❏ Yes
   ❏ Shelter or canopy
   ❏ Seating
   ❏ Interior waiting area
   ❏ Signage for bus schedules and routes
   ❏ Plantings
   ❏ Park-and-ride or commuter parking
   ❏ Direct enclosed pedestrian connection to transit
   ❏ Other (Describe): _____

   _____

D. Do you have any comments related to provision of transit at your center? _____

   _____

ADDITIONAL DATA ON THIS CENTER

Do you regularly collect parking counts during peak periods that you would be willing to share? (Data will be kept confidential and only used collectively) ❏ No   ❏ Yes

We are also requesting your assistance to conduct parked car counts during a Saturday in December. Information regarding this activity will be forthcoming.

If you have any questions or need assistance in completing this form, please contact John Dorsett with Walker Parking Consultants at 317-842-6890.

Thank you for completing this questionnaire.

Please return the completed form to:

Walker Parking Consultants
6602 E. 75th Street
Suite 210
Indianapolis, IN 46250

Appendix C
Parking Survey Results
General Questionnaire

	No. of Responses	Percentage of Respondents	Percentage of Total	
INFORMATION FOR THIS CENTER				
A. Shopping center location	113	23%	23%	Large Urban
	146	30%	30%	Urban
	186	39%	38%	Suburban
	31	6%	6%	Rural/Highway Non-urban
	7	2%	2%	Other
	483	100%	N/A	Subtotal
	7		1%	No Answer
	490		**100%**	**Total**
C. Type of shopping center	135	28%	28%	Neighborhood
	112	23%	23%	Community
	74	15%	15%	Regional
	102	21%	21%	Super Regional
	8	2%	2%	Fashion/Specialty
	27	6%	6%	Power
	16	3%	3%	Theme/Entertainment
	9	2%	2%	Outlet
	7	2%	2%	Other
	490	100%	N/A	Subtotal
	0		0%	No Answer
	490		**100%**	**Total**
PARKING AT THIS CENTER				
B. Are any of these spaces in a parking garage, deck or other structure?	416	87%	85%	No
	62	13%	13%	Yes
	478	100%	N/A	Subtotal
	12		2%	No Answer
	490		**100%**	**Total**
C. Is there any parking charge to the customer?	463	98%	94%	No
	9	2%	2%	Yes
	472	100%	N/A	Subtotal
	18		4%	No Answer
	490		**100%**	**Total**
Is there a parking validation program (by stores/tenants)?	421	98%	86%	No
	10	2%	2%	Yes
	431	100%	N/A	Subtotal
	59		12%	No Answer
	490		**100%**	**Total**

	No. of Responses	Percentage of Respondents	Percentage of Total	
Is there a valet parking program at this center?	407	96%	83%	No
	17	4%	4%	Yes
	424	100%	N/A	Subtotal
	66		13%	No Answer
	490		**100%**	**Total**
D. How many days per year is on-site parking fully occupied (over 95%) at any time during the day?	205	43%	42%	0
	11	2%	2%	1
	20	4%	4%	2
	29	6%	6%	3
	58	12%	12%	4-6
	28	6%	6%	7-9
	125	26%	25%	10+
	476	100%	N/A	Subtotal
	14		3%	No Answer
	490		**100%**	**Total**
This answer is based on:	57	13%	12%	Count
	380	87%	77%	Judgment
	437	100%	N/A	Subtotal
	53		11%	No Answer
	490		**100%**	**Total**
F. Is peak parking demand at this center usually associated with:	13	3%	3%	Special Event
	310	72%	63%	Seasonal/Holiday
	109	25%	22%	Combination
	432	100%	N/A	Subtotal
	58		12%	No Answer
	490		**100%**	**Total**
G. Does this shopping center participate in a local or Regional Transportation Management Association?	416	89%	85%	No
	54	11%	11%	Yes
	470	100%	N/A	Subtotal
	20		4%	No Answer
	490		**00%**	**Total**
H. Do shopping center tenant employees park on-site during off-peak seasons?	44	9%	9%	No
	428	91%	87%	Yes
	472	100%	N/A	Subtotal
	18		4%	No Answer
	490		**100%**	**Total**
If they park on site, are specific spaces reserved for employees?	267	66%	62%	No
	140	34%	33%	Yes
	407	100%	N/A	Subtotal
	21		5%	No Answer
	428		**100%**	**Total**

	No. of Responses	Percentage of Respondents	Percentage of Total	
Are employees ever charged for parking?	464	99%	95%	No
	7	1%	1%	Yes
	471	100%	N/A	Subtotal
	19		4%	No Answer
	490		**100%**	**Total**
Are shopping center employees asked to park in a different location during peak shopping times?	273	61%	56%	No
	175	39%	36%	Yes
	448	100%	N/A	Subtotal
	42		9%	No Answer
	490		**100%**	**Total**
Is violation of handicapped parking a common occurrence at your center?	375	82%	77%	No
	84	18%	17%	Yes
	459	100%	N/A	Subtotal
	31		6%	No Answer
	490		**100%**	**Total**
J. Are there spaces designated for compact cars?	375	82%	77%	No
	84	18%	17%	Yes
	459	100%	N/A	Subtotal
	31		6%	No Answer
	490		**100%**	**Total**
K. Do parkers from adjacent properties or land uses frequently park on shopping center property?	360	76%	73%	No
	113	24%	23%	Yes
	473	100%	N/A	Subtotal
	17		3%	No Answer
	490		**100%**	**Total**
2. Does this have a significant effect on parking availability for your shoppers?	95	78%	19%	No
	27	22%	6%	Yes
	122	100%	N/A	Subtotal
	368		75%	No Answer
	490		**100%**	**Total**
3. Has any action been taken to curb unauthorized parking?	51	36%	10%	No
	90	64%	18%	Yes
	141	100%	N/A	Subtotal
	349		71%	No Answer
	490		**100%**	**Total**

	No. of Responses	Percentage of Respondents	Percentage of Total	
M. Has there been any need to increase parking area, since the center opened, that was not associated with an expansion of tenant floor area?	361	88%	74%	No
	48	12%	10%	Yes
	409	100%	N/A	Subtotal
	81		16%	No Answer
	490		**100%**	**Total**

TRANSIT AT THIS CENTER

	No. of Responses	Percentage of Respondents	Percentage of Total	
A. Is there scheduled bus or train service to the shopping center area?	10			Train
	175			Bus
B. Do buses enter the center property?	304	63%	62%	No
	175	37%	36%	Yes
	479	100%	N/A	Subtotal
	11		2%	No Answer
	490		100%	Total
C. Which of the following amenities are provided for transit patrons?	131			Shelter or Canopy
	143			Seating
	35			Interior Waiting Area
	126			Signage for Bus Schedules and Routes
	54			Plantings
	22			Park-and-Ride or Commuter Parking
	2			Direct Enclosed Pedestrian Connection to Transit
	15			Other

ADDITIONAL DATA ON THIS CENTER

	No. of Responses	Percentage of Respondents	Percentage of Total	
Do you regularly collect parking counts during peak periods that you would be willing to share?	338	81%	69%	No
	79	19%	16%	Yes
	417	100%	N/A	Subtotal
	73		15%	No Answer
	490		**100%**	**Total**

ULI/ICSC Parking Requirements for Shopping Centers
Parked Car Survey—Data Collection Form

Name of Center ⬚

City/State ⬚

On-site Parking Capacity ⬚

Instructions:On Saturday, December 12, between 1:00 p.m. and 3:00 p.m., please record the following information, filling in all boxes on this form. This date and time frame are critical to the integrity of this study. Please fax the results of the survey to John Dorsett at (317) 577-6500.

No. of illegally parked cars ⬚

No. of empty parking spaces ⬚

No. of employees parking off site ⬚

Please contact John Dorsett at (317) 842-6890 if you have questions.
Walker Parking Consultants, ULI, and ICSC thank you for your participation.

Name of Center

_____

Location of Center

_____(City,State)

Owner/Manager

_____(Managing Company)

_____ (Center Manager)

_____

Center Type

_____(Community, Regional, etc.)

Basic Land Use Data

   Total Site Area

   _____Square feet

   Total Gross Leasable Area

   _____Square feet

   Total Vacant Area

   _____Square feet

   Total Occupied Area

   _____Square feet

Specific Site Characteristics

   Transit Service

   _____

   _____

   Surrounding Land Use

   _____

Parking Supply Data

   Parking Spaces

   _____

   Parking Index

   _____

Overall Tenant Data	Square Feet of GLA	Percent of Total GLA
Major Tenants		
_____	_____	_____
_____	_____	_____
_____	_____	_____
_____	_____	_____
Offices	_____	_____
Theaters	_____	_____
Food Service	_____	_____

Tenant Classifications	Number of Occupied Stores or Spaces	Square Feet of Total GLA*
General Merchandise	_____	_____
Food	_____	_____
Food Service	_____	_____
Clothing	_____	_____
Shoes	_____	_____
Home Furnishing	_____	_____
Home Appliance/Music	_____	_____
Building Materials/Garden	_____	_____
Auto Supplies/Service Station	_____	_____
Hobby/Special Interest	_____	_____
Gifts/Specialty	_____	_____
Liquor	_____	_____
Drugs	_____	_____
Other Retail	_____	_____
Personal Services	_____	_____
Recreation/Community	_____	_____
Financial	_____	_____
Offices	_____	_____
Other	_____	_____
Total	_____	_____

*Areas devoted to individual tenants are approximate.

Appendix F
Parking Ratio Calculations

1998 STUDY

Occupancy (GLA x 1,000)	Parking Supply Index	Design Hour Parking Space Demand	Design Hour Parking Demand Index
34.641	6.55293	130	3.75278
73.356	4.59403	224	3.05360
75.648	6.97970	329	4.34909
77.939	6.29980	285	3.65671
80.082	5.29302	236	2.94698
82.420	7.29192	375	4.54987
82.933	5.91311	368	4.43732
83.309	8.32129	418	5.01747[b]
83.403	5.92305	220	2.63779
84.053	6.26985	307	3.65246
85.174	6.99874	149	1.74936[b]
101.692	5.70305	298	2.93042
104.588	5.46908	405	3.87234
112.295	5.78525	421	3.74905[b]
127.250	[a]	498	3.91356
129.879	3.44564	192	1.47830[b]
134.376	6.54121	386	2.87254
145.104	4.89869	436	3.00474
146.122	8.17955	585	4.00350
146.484	5.09165	344	2.34838
148.294	6.59501	947	6.38596[b]
148.713	5.66191	636	4.27669[b]
150.888	7.93571	586	3.88368
168.000	2.70238	217	1.29167
172.023	5.28999	927	5.38881
209.040	6.38491	1097	5.24780
216.529	5.67637	988	4.56290
217.216	6.44913	965	4.44258[b]
233.796	5.70331	822	3.51589
243.094	4.67917	703	2.89189
245.477	6.34683	1556	6.33868
247.412	4.66815	892	3.60532[b]
252.643	3.76659	775	3.06757
256.392	7.01710	1176	4.58673

a   Center parking capacity not available.

b   Represents center where over 20 percent of floor area consists of a non-retail use (such as cinema, restaurant, entertainment, etc.).

1998 STUDY

Occupancy (GLA x 1,000)	Parking Supply Index	Design Hour Parking Space Demand	Design Hour Parking Demand Index
268.040	9.13490	1278	4.76795
269.237	7.37785	755	2.80422
272.623	4.66945	974	3.57270
273.632	6.21839	1521	5.55856
276.848	a	1021	3.68794
278.852	4.61953	1176	4.21729
297.030	7.68657	664	2.23546
317.419	5.67884	1140	3.59147
325.792	3.47171	655	2.01049
326.819	4.89673	953	2.91599
331.531	4.92865	755	2.27731
338.055	4.33066	1250	3.69762
345.000	a	770	2.23188
354.556	4.35756	1689	4.76370
359.941	5.98409	2307	6.40938
403.212	5.83756	1766	4.37983
417.937	6.16122	1242	2.97174
426.054	7.59344	2183	5.12376
441.199	5.09214	2065	4.68043
454.686	5.00125	1414	3.10984
463.332	6.46836	1913	4.12879
470.366	5.38458	2079	4.41996
475.734	6.76281	1138	2.39209
527.066	5.11321	1993	3.78131
534.766	5.07699	1835	3.43141
555.102	5.48548	3060	5.51250
572.000	3.53147	2262	3.95455
573.614	5.88375	2548	4.44201
588.732	6.57376	3285	5.57979
588.900	4.58966	1606	2.72712[b]
613.907	5.92187	3526	5.74354
615.460	5.86963	2768	4.49745
628.245	a	1514	2.40989
629.476	5.40132	2455	3.90007

a   Center parking capacity not available.

b   Represents center where over 20 percent of floor area consists of a non-retail use (such as cinema, restaurant, entertainment, etc.).

1998 STUDY

Occupancy (GLA x 1,000)	Parking Supply Index	Design Hour Parking Space Demand	Design Hour Parking Demand Index
634.200	5.49038	2123	3.34752
635.189	5.46325	3307	5.20632
656.402	5.86531	3010	4.58560
680.700	5.93507	2923	4.29411
682.799	4.33009	2224	3.25718
684.435	4.69146	3211	4.69146
685.003	6.49486	4389	6.40727
687.689	7.76514	4232	6.15394
710.238	2.81596	1789	2.51887
720.000	6.22222	1586	2.20278
726.445	5.17089	3860	5.31355
727.445	6.03894	2395	3.29235
735.121	8.97660	4501	6.12280
738.074	6.84393	3781	5.12279
743.000	5.79538	2709	3.64603
743.231	6.49965	4475	6.02101
745.819	5.89694	4136	5.54558
780.678	6.37168	3799	4.86628
781.550	5.06174	3265	4.17760
787.694	4.82368	3588	4.55507
794.074	5.99314	4019	5.06124
800.000	5.62500	3513	4.39125
800.412	5.35287	2481	3.09965
808.078	4.56808	3180	3.93526
810.500	6.66379	4435	5.47193
813.261	5.95135	4540	5.58246
813.415	8.63112	2025	2.48950[b]
838.793	[a]	2015	2.40226
839.677	5.00076	4002	4.76612
842.347	[a]	3829	4.54563
860.000	5.17674	2855	3.31977
862.924	4.76869	2292	2.65609
866.767	5.54941	4171	4.81214

a   Center parking capacity not available.

b   Represents center where over 20 percent of floor area consists of a non-retail use (such as cinema, restaurant, entertainment, etc.).

1998 STUDY

Occupancy (GLA x 1,000)	Parking Supply Index	Design Hour Parking Space Demand	Design Hour Parking Demand Index
878.316	5.65037	1883	2.14388
883.309	4.46024	3027	3.42689
884.067	5.09011	5060	5.72355
893.034	7.03864	4267	4.77809
901.660	3.29503	3341	3.70539
903.068	4.52458	4043	4.47696
903.396	4.93034	4073	4.50854
931.854	4.36227	3541	3.79995
941.488	5.22046	4699	4.99104
949.637	18.97106	4997	5.26201
970.000	4.84845	4139	4.26701
972.579	4.51891	4461	4.58677
977.478	4.58488	4402	4.50343
998.209	4.80861	5101	5.11015
1001.000	5.23477	3902	3.89810
1008.266	5.66021	5813	5.76534
1018.637	5.10915	4687	4.60125
1029.172	5.56272	3762	3.65537
1030.610	5.38103	5224	5.06884
1035.825	5.26633	4875	4.70639
1036.468	5.63452	5666	5.46664
1052.946	5.84835	6176	5.86545
1054.774	4.71001	5088	4.82378
1057.851	5.30434	5600	5.29375
1071.634	5.66459	4915	4.58645
1071.651	5.18079	5092	4.75155
1078.568	6.03764	5151	4.77578
1086.048	4.40981	4188	3.85618
1101.077	5.09592	5277	4.79258
1103.248	5.89169	4214	3.81963
1106.746	4.57377	3741	3.38018
1108.061	5.13607	5432	4.90226
1117.801	4.95795	5244	4.69135
1125.557	5.33186	5045	4.48223

a   Center parking capacity not available.

b   Represents center where over 20 percent of floor area consists of a non-retail use (such as cinema, restaurant, entertainment, etc.).

Appendix F (*cont.*)
Parking Ratio Calculations

1998 STUDY

Occupancy (GLA x 1,000)	Parking Supply Index	Design Hour Parking Space Demand	Design Hour Parking Demand Index
1130.288	5.55079	5502	4.86779
1143.796	3.97161	5314	4.64593
1148.145	5.67933	5025	4.37662
1154.840	5.22847	5292	4.58245
1165.823	5.42261	5931	5.08739
1174.001	5.02533	5607	4.77598
1176.095	5.73588	6221	5.28954
1183.690	19.69732	3154	2.66455
1192.541	5.31470	6578	5.51595
1242.159	5.87053	6341	5.10482
1250.000	4.87500	5920	4.73600
1267.058	5.09567	6390	5.04318
1286.323	5.04677	6330	4.92100
1291.896	6.36131	5197	4.02277
1300.000	4.84615	6348	4.88308
1301.199	5.95790	6552	5.03536
1307.568	a	5590	4.27511
1312.174	6.02249	4440	3.38370
1319.500	5.45231	7088	5.37173
1366.521	5.23080	7379	5.39984
1370.045	5.68932	7503	5.47646
1371.204	5.83866	7743	5.64686
1387.013	5.66035	7269	5.24076
1403.642	5.66802	6845	4.87660
1427.104	4.79376	6650	4.65979
1510.708	4.66801	6158	4.07623
1531.972	4.68155	7240	4.72593
1543.396	4.37708	4931	3.19490
1544.000	4.66321	5960	3.86010
1625.374	4.61494	6973	4.29009
1700.000	a	5715	3.36176
1705.272	4.48081	7356	4.31368
1850.903	4.86249	4325	2.33670[b]
2384.388	5.25901	10287	4.31431

a   Center parking capacity not available.

b   Represents center where over 20 percent of floor area consists of a non-retail use (such as cinema, restaurant, entertainment, etc.).

1980 STUDY

Occupancy (GLA x 1,000)	Parking Supply Index	Design Hour Parking Space Demand	Design Hour Parking Demand Index
27.564	7.43724	185	6.71165
36.498	5.31536	134	3.67143
43.376	5.44080	106	2.44375
43.400	7.39631	148	3.41014
48.018	3.72777	188	3.91520
58.410	7.46448	118	2.02020
58.707	6.83053	427	7.27341
59.456	8.08956	184	3.09473
61.883	6.80316	145	2.34313
63.664	6.00025	179	2.81164
63.800	4.09091	239	3.74608
64.701	5.25494	174	2.68929
65.000	5.15385	185	2.84615
67.257	4.18232	460	6.83944
68.000	4.47059	272	4.00000
68.030	4.11583	196	2.88108
68.870	6.04037	289	4.19631
73.949	5.93652	115	1.55513
74.880	7.63889	273	3.64583
77.370	6.70803	276	3.56727
78.627	5.75682	359	4.56586
81.644	3.82147	218	2.67013
82.166	6.31648	265	3.22518
82.655	6.17023	240	2.90364
85.075	5.24243	237	2.78578
89.701	8.28580	397	4.43156
90.000	4.24444	196	2.17778
92.619	6.46736	401	4.32947
94.389	5.38198	303	3.21012
94.950	8.18325	524	5.51869
101.832	5.11652	316	3.10315
104.940	3.76406	368	3.50677
107.000	4.74766	416	3.88785
107.100	4.43511	402	3.75350
109.000	5.76147	311	2.85321

1980 STUDY

Occupancy (GLA x 1,000)	Parking Supply Index	Design Hour Parking Space Demand	Design Hour Parking Demand Index
109.111	3.60184	147	1.34725
110.000	5.54545	269	2.44545
110.170	5.86367	453	4.11183
112.237	4.28557	349	3.10949
113.000	4.34783	422	3.73451
116.550	7.16431	366	3.14028
117.479	4.95408	528	4.49442
127.048	4.44714	309	2.43215
146.141	5.65208	541	3.70190
148.000	4.00000	412	2.78378
160.000	7.04375	716	4.47500
160.240	5.48050	368	2.29656
170.391	8.16358	337	1.97780
172.458	7.72362	1,165	6.75527
176.877	5.34835	904	5.11090
180.000	4.58333	703	3.90556
202.444	5.91982	944	4.66302
202.500	3.40741	557	2.75062
221.060	6.52764	1,378	6.23360
221.508	5.06528	1,068	4.82150
241.200	5.70481	1,382	5.72968
248.937	4.53127	903	3.62742
250.663	6.18759	1,090	4.34847
268.199	5.85759	859	3.20285
272.700	7.04437	1,587	5.81958
283.273	6.83793	1,007	3.55487
296.120	7.95623	1,644	5.55180
320.000	6.58750	1,457	4.55312
323.500	5.70943	1,173	3.62597
334.435	5.51378	1,712	5.11908
337.092	6.27425	1,218	3.61326
350.306	4.80437	1,702	4.85861
381.282	7.28070	2,690	7.05515
400.634	8.20949	1,718	4.28820
410.091	7.40811	2,568	6.26202
417.344	4.79618	2,371	5.68116

1980 STUDY

Occupancy (GLA x 1,000)	Parking Supply Index	Design Hour Parking Space Demand	Design Hour Parking Demand Index
420.621	6.15281	2,285	5.43244
429.000	4.44522	1,182	2.75524
429.845	3.45706	1,512	3.51755
432.040	7.00398	1,634	3.78206
440.472	5.56903	2,267	5.14675
456.588	7.39178	2,239	4.90376
464.666	4.60546	2,070	4.45481
464.920	5.41168	2,406	5.17508
467.565	4.54910	2,138	4.57263
497.234	5.33424	1,720	3.45914
523.421	6.39256	2,590	4.94822
527.693	7.51194	3,094	5.86326
529.856	4.86925	2,235	4.21813
530.000	5.45283	3,166	5.97358
538.000	5.78996	3,004	5.58364
550.000	6.16786	2,741	4.98364
555.000	5.60901	3,380	6.09009
558.035	7.53358	3,531	6.32756
587.595	7.41667	4,168	7.09332
593.355		3,952	6.66043
600.000	5.68000	3,408	5.68000
602.210	4.28089	2,972	4.93515
607.660	4.85966	3,116	5.12790
620.000	5.71935	3,432	5.53548
620.730	6.62449	2,743	4.41901
630.000	7.61905	4,800	7.61905
650.610	5.61014	3,564	5.44795
667.390	5.52448	3,482	5.21732
687.530	7.29710	3,329	4.84195
687.90	3.69240	1,888	2.74458
692.72	6.20888	4,182	6.03710
700.00	6.00000	4,029	5.75571
701.91	5.58189	3,544	5.04906
702.18	8.18445	5,271	7.50657
708.70	5.49930	2,884	4.06945
720.00	4.53472	3,149	4.37361

1980 STUDY

Occupancy (GLA x 1,000)	Parking Supply Index	Design Hour Parking Space Demand	Design Hour Parking Demand Index
724.30	6.52216	3,202	4.42082
729.53	5.95178	4,301	5.89558
733.04	4.71868	3,093	4.21939
733.13	5.37424	3,973	5.41925
735.90	5.59995	4,121	5.59995
739.89	5.83599	4,390	5.93331
758.43	5.07496	2,512	3.31211
765.76	8.46611	4,881	6.37407
803.91	5.97827	4,453	5.53917
810.50	5.38680	4,321	5.33128
819.26	5.43173	4,223	5.15465
828.69	4.87638	4,180	5.04411
831.09	5.29428	3,812	4.58677
841.33	5.55310	5,291	6.28884
841.33	5.48178	7,771	9.23654
844.80	5.68297	5,461	6.46422
853.04	6.68875	4,093	4.75821
865.35	5.68210	5,465	6.31537
871.87	4.42040	3,420	3.92262
889.03	4.26083	2,955	3.32385
905.79	5.54988	5,087	5.61612
914.93	5.67147	4,191	4.58068
947.00	5.49102	4,693	4.95565
947.51	6.33235	5,076	5.35717
950.00	2.36316	1,884	1.98316
955.57	3.88356	3,916	4.09809
974.63	5.62777	5,688	5.83605
978.00	4.60123	4,225	4.32004
992.27	5.86331	6,446	6.49620
998.36	5.90969	6,447	6.45759
1014.82	6.71624	5,456	5.37643
1015.09	5.91081	6,410	6.31471
1032.43	3.94312	4,053	3.92568
1038.93	Not applicable	4,437	Not applicable
1048.00	5.82061	5,619	5.36164

1980 STUDY

Occupancy (GLA x 1,000)	Parking Supply Index	Design Hour Parking Space Demand	Design Hour Parking Demand Index
1061.29	5.54327	5,759	5.42644
1104.46	5.79377	3,429	3.10468
1132.36	5.00019	5,497	4.85448
1199.98	5.80591	6,809	5.67424
1200.00	5.37833	4,369	3.64083
1289.32	5.09337	3,755	2.91238
1438.00	5.64743	7,513	5.22462
1469.78	4.57076	5,883	4.00264

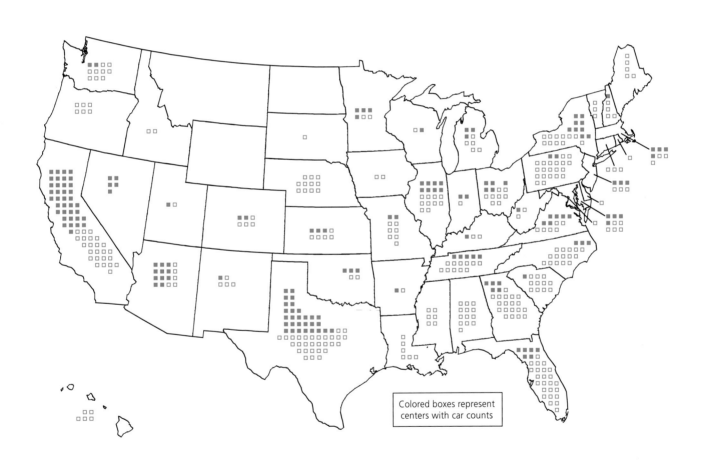

Colored boxes represent
centers with car counts

Carousel
Center

Independence
Mall

Santa
Monica Place

Castleton
Square

Plaza Frontenac

St. Charles
Towne Plaza

Chapel
Hills Mall

Showcase

Camelback
Colonnade

Irvine Spectrum

Village Fair

Lakepointe
Crossing

Shadybrook
Mall

Cielo Vista Mall

Plaza Del Sol

To establish December 12, 1998, as the day best representing the 20th busiest hour, detailed data were obtained from 32 shopping centers that collect continuous data via the following mechanisms:

- Pedestrian counting devices at entries/exits
- Vehicular counting devices on entry roads that capture inbound vehicular traffic counts
- Parking access and revenue control equipment that tracks parking activity.

In short, much more extensive data are available, at least for large centers, than were available during either of the two previous studies.

For the survey conducted in 1997, 16 centers provided hourly pedestrian/vehicular traffic data. Based on a review of data from these 16 centers, the time period that best captured conditions representing the 20th busiest hour was between the hours of 1:00 p.m. and 3:00 p.m. on the second Saturday before the week of Christmas.

To best determine conditions representing the 20th busiest hour, an analysis of the 16 centers providing hourly pedestrian/vehicular traffic volumes was conducted. Since the 20th busiest hour fell on 11 different days, a range including the reported 18th through 22nd busiest hours was evaluated for each of the 16 centers. The variance in

daily traffic volumes representing days capturing the 18th versus the 22nd busiest hour was small—3.1 percent. Based on this evaluation, Saturday, December 13, 1997, was the day most often capturing the 18th through the 22nd busiest hour. As shown in Table 15, Saturday, December 13, 1997, was represented 11 times out of a possible 80 (16 centers x 5 positions—18, 19, 20, 21, 22 per center) chances.

An analysis of daily pedestrian/vehicular traffic volumes for the 32 centers collecting daily data provided further evidence that the 20th busiest hour is best captured on the second Saturday before the week of Christmas, in this case, December 12, 1998. Moreover, the 1980 *Parking Requirements for Shopping Centers* study used the second Saturday before the week of Christmas as a data collection day,

Table 15
18th–22nd Busiest Hour for 16 Centers

| | Number of Centers with: | | | | | |
Date	18th Busiest Hour	19th Busiest Hour	20th Busiest Hour	21st Busiest Hour	22nd Busiest Hour	Total 18th–22nd Busiest Hour
12/13/97	1	2	1	5	2	11
12/21/97	2	3	3	0	1	9
12/20/97	1	3	1	1	2	8
12/26/97	2	2	1	1	0	6
12/23/97	0	0	4	0	1	5
12/14/97	1	1	1	1	1	5
12/22/97	1	0	1	1	2	5
12/6/97	0	0	0	3	1	4
12/24/97	2	1	0	0	1	4
11/27/98	0	1	1	0	2	4
11/28/98	0	1	1	0	2	4
12/27/97	1	0	0	1	0	2
12/19/97	2	0	0	0	0	2
11/21/98	1	0	0	1	0	2
2/14/98	1	0	0	1	0	2
11/22/98	0	1	0	0	0	1
12/28/97	0	0	0	0	1	1
12/29/97	1	0	0	0	0	1
11/7/98	0	1	0	0	0	1
8/22/98	0	0	1	0	0	1
12/7/97	0	0	1	0	0	1
1/2/98	0	0	0	1	0	1

providing yet another reason to select this Saturday as a data collection day for this study.

It is extremely difficult to identify the collective 20th busiest hour for a group of centers. In the case of the 16 centers that provided hourly pedestrian/vehicular traffic volumes for the year 1997, 16 different hours were identified as the 20th busiest hour.

The parking and pedestrian/vehicular traffic data collected from the 32 centers were evaluated to identify the busiest days of parking and traffic conditions and, ultimately, to support the use of December 13, 1997, as a day approximating the 20th busiest hour. In 1997, the 20th busiest hour most frequently fell on Saturday, December 13. Therefore, the second Saturday preceding the week of Christmas was established as the date to maximize the probability of capturing the 20th busiest hour. Consequently, the 1998 Parked Car Survey was conducted on Saturday, December 12, 1998.

Table 16 lists the 18 busiest days based on parking and pedestrian/traffic data from the 32 centers. The top ten days of volume were ranked for each of the 32 centers. Only 18 days were represented by at least two centers as having one of the top ten positions. The day most frequently represented as the busiest was Tuesday, December 23, 1997.

The following is how Table 16 should be read:

Read across the row labeled Tuesday, December 23, 1997. Eleven of the 32 centers reported December 23, 1997, as their busiest day measured by parking and pedestrian/vehicular traffic volumes. Three of the 32 centers reported it as their second busiest day. Four of

the 32 centers reported it as their third busiest day, etc.

After the day best representing the 20th busiest hour was determined, the *time* of day needed to be resolved. The 25 busiest hours were examined for each of the 16 centers that provided hourly parking data. Of the 400 total hours examined (16 centers x 25 busiest

Table 16
Top Parking and Pedestrian/Vehicular Traffic Days

Rank		Date	1st	2nd	3rd	4th	5th	6th	7th	8th	9th	10th	Total
1st	Tues.	12/23/97	11	3	4	4	2	5	1	0	1	1	32
2nd	Sat.	12/20/97	4	8	8	4	4	2	1	1	0	0	32
3rd	Sat.	12/13/97	6	5	4	5	3	3	4	0	1	0	31
4th	Mon.	12/22/97	2	7	5	5	6	3	1	1	0	1	31
5th	Fri.	12/26/97	3	3	5	3	7	4	3	2	0	0	30
6th	Sat.	12/6/97	0	0	0	4	0	5	2	6	3	3	23
7th	Fri.	12/19/97	0	0	1	0	2	1	4	4	4	4	20
8th	Fri.	11/28/97	2	1	0	4	1	2	1	0	2	0	13
9th	Fri.	12/12/97	0	0	0	0	1	0	1	3	2	6	13
10th	Sun.	12/21/97	0	2	0	1	0	1	1	2	3	3	13
11th	Sat.	12/27/97	1	0	0	0	0	1	3	3	2	1	11
12th	Wed.	12/24/97	0	1	1	1	2	0	1	1	2	1	10
13th	Thurs.	12/18/97	0	0	1	0	1	1	2	2	1	2	10
14th	Fri.	11/27/98	2	0	0	1	0	1	1	1	0	0	6
15th	Wed.	12/17/97	0	0	0	0	0	1	0	0	0	3	4
16th	Sat.	11/29/97	0	0	0	0	0	0	1	0	2	0	3
17th	Fri.	2/14/97	0	0	0	0	1	0	0	0	0	1	2
18th	Sat.	11/28/98	0	0	1	0	0	0	1	0	0	0	2

Note: The only days that were included in this table are days that ranked in the top ten inbound traffic for at least two centers. Data were obtained from 32 centers.

hours), 67 percent occurred between 1:00 and 3:00 p.m. Furthermore, as shown in Figure 11, the 20th busiest hour was analyzed for each of these 16 centers, and 69 percent fell between the hours of 1:00 and 3:00 p.m. Therefore, the Parked Car Survey was scheduled to be conducted on Saturday, December 12, 1998, between 1:00 and 3:00 p.m.

Figure 11
Distribution of 25 Busiest
Hours for 16 Centers

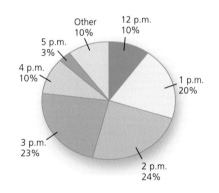

Note: The center types are defined in Chapter 5.